Consecrating Our Waits

Consecrating Our Waits

MICHELLE L. MARTIN

IZZARD INK™
PUBLISHING

Editing: Catherine Garrett and Heather Green
Design: Angie Lawrence

ISBN:
ebook 9781630729103
paperback 9781630729110

Library of Congress Control Number: 2016956021

Izzard Ink Publishing Company
PO Box 522251
Salt Lake City, Utah 84152
www.izzardink.com

ACKNOWLEDGMENTS

To my angel parents who have guided me all along the way!

To Heavenly Father and all His angels who have helped me,
inspired me, whispered in my ear,
and sometimes told me exactly what to write!

To Catherine Garrett and Heather Green for their countless
hours of kindness, love, and editing!

To Angie Lawrence for your creative brilliance, compassion
and generous time you spent designing this book!

To Julia Hammond, a very warm thank you for
your inspired forward!

To Kara Arnold Applegate and Steven Sharp Nelson, thank
you for your time and encouragement!

To my wonderful friends who have contributed to the
realization of this book: Kathy Robertson, Terra Taylor,
Cathy Larson-Taylor, Katrina Troutman, Ken and Kendra
Moss, Camille Kennard, Heather Rothey Lyon, David
McCallister, Drew Johnson, Cara Baldree, Blake and
Keltson Howell, and Johnathan Newbold.

This book is dedicated to my nieces and nephews.

CONTENTS

FORWARD

My mother always told me that good things come to those who wait. Even with the anticipation of good things, waiting is difficult. Making that time count is vital, especially when the wait is extensive.

In *Consecrating Our Waits*, Michelle L. Martin offers wonderful ways to focus our lives outside of ourselves; to realize greater purpose in our lives, especially when our lives take a different path than we had planned. She has shared wonderful experiences, often personal and poignant, that remind us of the opportunities that await us when we put aside our own concerns and step forward to realize the wonders of this life that God has given us.

We journey with Michelle to the mountains of Honduras where she joins with others to bring smiles to the children of San Pedro Sula and their families. She shares tender moments with her sweet mother as she faced a premature death. The depth of her love for friends, those known and unknown, is witnessed as she shares meaningful visiting teaching experiences. We ache with her for those who struggle with challenges far beyond their control and gain a greater appreciation for what we have here in our own country. Being reminded of our responsibility, the needs that surround us, and the covenants we have made strengthens our resolve and gives us the impetus needed to "go about doing good." I am grateful to Michelle for her powerful example.

More than twenty years ago, I started experiencing problems with chronic pain, making it very difficult for me to even get up and face the day. Having to depend on my family and others for help was humiliating. I was angry with my situation and desperately sad about life in general. Many treatments were tried without success. Feeling defeated and like I could not be productive, I spent days on the couch doing little more than feeling sorry for myself.

I was waiting for my life to change; waiting to feel better. For a very long time, I prayed to be healed. I received priesthood blessings, having faith that I would indeed be restored. My health didn't change. Eventually, I realized that I had a choice. I could choose to stay on the couch and be consumed in myself, or I could get up and focus outside of myself.

As my focus changed away from myself, my testimony and my faith strengthened. My energy increased and I felt purpose and joy in life. Just as we learn in this book, newfound determination enabled me to volunteer, to serve in demanding callings, to spend extra time with those in need, to be a more dedicated visiting teacher, and to show gratitude to the "ministering angels" who had so generously served me. There were opportunities all around me to serve, to love, and to see the hand of God in my life. Facing my "Goliath" was no longer impossible. I have been and continue to be richly blessed by my Heavenly Father as I do my part. Those who read this book will find it useful and uplifting in their search for fulfillment during challenging waiting periods.

Consecrating Our Waits teaches us to refocus our lives in positive, meaningful ways, realizing that the twists and turns, the experiences off the beaten path are the most precious and powerful. We were not put on this earth as observers, but as participants. There is no joy in waiting, but there is great joy in consecrating that time to our Father and His Son. Good things do indeed come to those who wait.

Michelle is a woman of integrity who lives her life ever thoughtful of others and their needs. Her compassion and inner strength combine to make her a powerful force for good in this life.

I join her in testifying that our Father in Heaven and His Son Jesus Christ care deeply for us and desire the greatest joy for us. May we seek it and find it as we consecrate our lives to Their service.

—Julia Hammond

CHAPTER 1

Bringing the Smile of Jesus to Others

"And it came to pass that Jesus blessed them as they did pray unto him; and his countenance did smile upon them, and the light of his countenance did shine upon them, and behold they were as white as the countenance and also the garments of Jesus; and behold the whiteness thereof did exceed all the whiteness, yea, even there could be nothing upon earth so white as the whiteness thereof." (3 Nephi 19:25)

We are all waiting for something to happen in life—waiting to graduate, waiting to get married, to go on a mission, to get healthy, to be healed, waiting to have a baby, waiting to die, waiting to find a job, waiting for a raise, waiting for someone to come home from a mission, waiting to retire, and many more *waits* in life! One of my life-long best friends, Kathy, was recently diagnosed with leukemia; consequently, she had to wait to see if there was a life-saving match for a bone marrow transplant. First, they tried her siblings—no match, then the national registry—no match; a few months later—the international registry—finally...a perfect match from someone on the other side of the world in Eastern Europe. While she was waiting, praying, and hoping for this miracle, we were all praying, fasting, and hoping right along with her! This book is to suggest that while we wait in life, let us *consecrate this wait!*

Three months after Kathy received her transplant, I was able to travel back to Oregon and visit with her. I was so impressed with how she had *consecrated this waiting period.* She had such a strong spirit of faith about her. You knew that through this furnace of affliction she truly had strengthened her relationship with the Savior and her Heavenly Father! I felt

simply uplifted by just being with her. She said to me, "I know I need to write down all these experiences so when I am better I don't forget what the Lord has taught me."

Mortality and 'times of waiting and delay' can sometimes cause physical achy pain to our hearts and souls. It is at times like these that we must dig deep, soul searching, plead for heaven—even if it feels like no one is there! The Prince of Peace will never turn His back on us. We must ask for help in the thick of pleadings and searching. He is there! Seek His counsel and guidance in the ways you can *consecrate these waits.* As hard as it is to understand sometimes, I know *there is purpose in our waits.* I promise there is comfort to be found, emotional healing to be discovered, and relief in His Atonement and grace! We are taught this in the beautiful gospel truth of the Hymn *Come, Ye Disconsolate*:

"Come, ye disconsolate, where'er ye languish;
Come to the mercy seat, fervently kneel.
Here bring your wounded hearts;
here tell your anguish.
Earth has no sorrow that heav'n cannot heal."

In my own personal life, it is the 'waiting to be married' that can sometimes be heavy on my heart. Consequently, I find that reaching outside of myself to local service or humanitarian trips helps me to feel like I've dedicated this 'wait time' to God's purposes. Since I don't have children of my own to send on missions, I can serve by going on a dental/medical humanitarian trip in Central America, helping prospective missionaries get all their medical and dental work done. I felt that one particular trip I took in November of 2014 was a way that I could help hasten the Lord's work. That year I had the great privilege to join the extraordinary humanitarian group *Smiles for Central America* to San Pedro Sula, Honduras. This team of dental and medical professionals, and other volunteers, travel to several countries in Central America twice a year to provide services to prospective missionaries. This wonderful non-profit group and team of volunteers also provide community service in the city they are serving in. While there, I provided oral hygiene care to many of the young men and women. Our group saw a total of 660 young adults in preparation for their missions.

Before we arrived, they took a local Stake Center in Honduras and turned the entire building into a clinic—AMAZING!! All of the pew seats were removed and portable dental equipment was brought in. It will vary from city to city of how many volunteers they have. Our group consisted of 21 dentists, 4 dental hygienists, 5 endodontists, 1 orthodontist, 5 oral surgeons, 5 doctors, and 1 physician assistant. These services help ensure that these missionaries are healthy when they leave to their assigned areas in the world, and not have to worry about preexisting conditions like a toothache. ☺ Many of the young men and women we served had never been to a medical or dental professional. Despite the fact that some were scared, I found they were all so grateful to receive this free care that was given to them! They kept saying, "*Gracias*" or "*Thank you*" in broken English.

There was a local team in San Pedro Sula that provided support for our equipment, food, translation needs, and other things. Every clinician that needed a translator was provided one. I was touched by my interactions with so many of these beautiful young people, but three in particular made a lasting imprint on my heart! ☺ Marcella was 15 years old and spoke very good English. She was such a hard worker and very fun. We would listen to Salsa music from my phone and would dance around in the clinic; it didn't take long before a few were calling me the dancing hygienist! ☺ Her parents were part of the local team that helped us out so much and were true angels! Marcella and her brother, Sam, both translated in the clinic and worked so hard with a "go get 'em" mentality, I know that will carry them far in life.

Andrea was another translator I fell in love with because of her positive infectious personality, her great English skills helped me tremendously too! She had recently gotten home from a mission in Salt Lake City. She is now happily married to another returned missionary she had dated prior to her mission. ☺ Joseph, who had served a mission in Guatemala, had been a recipient of these free services four years earlier before his mission. Now, he wanted to give back to those who had helped him in his life. He had begun his studies to be a dentist. This young man simply said he wanted to be in a position to help others, like he had been helped. He was taking advantage of the Perpetual Education Fund where young adults are given financial assistance to afford college tuition and then pay it back upon completion of their education; very much like a micro-credit program. I felt such love for these wonderful young Honduran people who come from humble backgrounds, and yet radiate such happiness!

One of my favorite days of this whole trip was on Sunday. We went to church in San Pedro Sula and brought each family and child some fun things made with love! It was like an early Christmas for them!

A few of the more memorable gifts we gave them were listed specifically in my personal journal:

- For those over the age of 12 they received a journal.

- For those boys and men over the age of 12 they received a shirt and tie.

- For the women over the age of 18 they got beautiful handmade quilts.

- For those over the age of 12 they got handmade jewelry (youth from the states made all of the jewelry).

- Soccer balls for the youth, play clothes for the young children, they were so excited to put on their Zorro costumes and the little princess outfits. It was so awesome to watch them—it was like Christmas morning for these children.

- I loved this so much and enjoyed seeing these church members so happy! Family photos were taken for each family, which were printed and framed for them that very day! ☺ These parents were so touched that they shed tears of joy; for some of these families, it was their first picture taken together.

- I was assigned to the 'boutique' room and got to hand out jewelry to the women 18+, they were so happy and grateful to receive these gifts. When we were boarding our shuttles to leave, we saw many kids laughing, kicking soccer balls, and wearing Zorro costumes and princess dresses. ☺

- It was awesome to mingle with these families; it was hot and humid during sacrament with lots of mosquitoes, yet we felt right at home with these beautiful saints! They had fans on the ceiling and open windows (no air conditioning)—I truly loved this day!!!

Later on that evening we attended a meeting that was televised and shared via satellite with many LDS congregations throughout Honduras. The purpose of this meeting was to testify of Jesus Christ and to encourage the young people: young men 16 and older and young women 17 and older could take advantage of this free service to help prepare those who wanted to go on a full-time mission to attend. Many wonderful things were shared and testified about at this meeting; it was inspiring for all who attended. There was specifically one who spoke which to me was life changing! He was a General Authority of the Seventy who lived in Central America. His name was Elder Jose L. Alonso. He spoke about what we were doing there in Honduras on what they called a 'Brigade' and what our purpose was. He was truly filled with the Spirit. He told them we had come on our own time and dime. The following is my brief paraphrasing from my journal:

He quoted from 3 Nephi and asked, "Why did the Savior visit the American continent?" He explained that Christ blessed them on the American continent. With the power of the Holy Ghost, he shared the part that says, *"His smile was upon them—the light of His countenance was upon them." Elder Alonso strongly testified that HE lives! He is loving and knows us by name! He also said, "I testify HE knows how to smile! HE is real—the smiles of HIS face was with them from the Book of Mormon!"* He shared great appreciation for the Atonement of Jesus Christ—that those in our group from *Smiles for Central America* are here to share their time, talents, love, and are here to bring the smile of Jesus! They are here to share the plain manifestation of Jesus because HE loves us! *The Savior purified those from the Book of Mormon because of their faith—He prayed without ceasing, again, HE SMILED UPON THEM!* Tongue cannot express the words that HE prayed—Elder Alonso then invited the youth to kneel down that night and ask the Lord..."Do you love me?" He said, "You need to have confirmation from the Spirit. I testify that those who are with this group will bring you the smile of Jesus!" ☺ (I was so humbled to hear this—it changed the spirit of our group and the tone for the rest of the trip—we were on the Lord's errand!!!) Later on that evening (either in a talk or in a prayer), our group was blessed that our bodies could go beyond our capacity, our eyes that they could see with our head lights, that we'd be blessed beyond our capabilities!! *All of these blessings were fulfilled!!!* He continued on…"God has answers to life's problems! These people that are here will love you and bring you the love and smile of Jesus to the people of Honduras!" ☺

It was amazing as the week went on. We were blessed way beyond our capacity in order to provide long days of clinical work. It was very long hours and challenging ergonomically. A few more notes from my journal about the many wonderful opportunities we had to bring the smile of Jesus to others:

Monday, November 24, 2014: Another amazing day! Everyone in our group is invited to go on a mini human-itarian trip. Today my group got to go on ours. We went to a newborn clinic in town at a local hospital. I got to snuggle with lots of babies! There were two units: one was an adolescent unit with teen moms and the other was one for moms over 18 years old. We gave everyone newborn kits and they were so appreciative. We told them these kits were made with love and given to them with love! This was such a joy to hand them out. Each mother was also given a stuffed animal for the baby. The newborn kits had diapers, onesies, a receiving blanket, booties, handmade hats, and beautiful big handmade quilts! All these babies were so precious and all had so much hair! ☺ Right after the women delivered their babies, they were immediately whisked away and carried to a huge recovery room where they were placed on basic sheets; anything else they needed they must have brought themselves (clothes for the baby, nursing bra, etc.). These ladies were so happy to receive the newborn kits!! ☺ We also saw the NICU clinic with maybe half the resources we have in the USA. Kathy was our translator today; she is wonderful and was a fantastic translator, she served a mission in Ecuador. Kathy is a high school teacher, she was so delightful and is from San Pedro Sula. This was such a wonderful trip and day.

The woman in this photo is Terra Taylor, a friend and also a fellow dental hygienist that I met on the trip. On her mini humanitarian trip, she visited a children's hospital and saw children that had cancer. The group brought them fun toys and gadgets and the children absolutely loved it. In Terra's words, "The opportunity to visit, serve and touch these beautiful and precious souls was a choice blessing in my life. The recipients expressed heartfelt gratitude that I have only felt while serving on these humanitarian trips. Their gifts to me are so much greater than anything I could ever give or do for them. They are real people who touched my heart with a profound feeling of love, joy, appreciation, and healing that I hope to pass on to the world." More from my journal from that day:

Today at the clinic, we saw a total of 165 prospected missionaries. I saw so many wonderful kids today; some were anxious, some excited to be able to get all their paperwork done for free, some newly baptized, one that has been living on the streets until a few months ago when he met the missionaries and joined the Church and now is excited to go on a mission. This was so inspiring and amazing to me! I remember when I was baptized—I knew immediately that I too wanted to serve a mission!

I also had Marcella and Joseph today (other fantastic translators). ☺ VERY TIRED. This trip was so awesome—but we did have long days, and using a headlight for our dental work made it very challenging ergonomically.

Tuesday, November 25, 2014: Today was our busiest day, but it was an awesome day; we saw a total of *207 kids today*. My neck and back are super sore and tired—it was a 16-hour day. I know Heavenly Father blessed us beyond our capacity today for sure. Even our equipment was *not* made to run that many hours without breaking down. I also really loved working with all our amazing translators!

Wednesday, November 26, 2014: Last day of clinic today. We saw 98 and *a total of 660 patients for the whole week! That is simply a miracle!* There were 21 dentists, 6 oral surgeons, 5 endodontists, 5 MD's, 1 PA, many nurses—it was absolutely amazing helping *the hastening of the work of the Lord!!!*

When these young, prospective missionaries left the Stake Center, all of their mission paperwork was done and ready to turn into their Bishop! ☺

I am grateful for opportunities to serve others and to think outside myself while enduring my *waits* in life! Think about your life and how you can best *consecrate your waits!* We are all at different places in life; whether it's a painful wait or pushing through the mundane in life I promise there is help from heaven, work to do, and an abundant life to live!

To quote Elder Neal A. Maxwell; "Mortality involves teeth to be brushed, beds to be made, cars to be repaired, diapers to be changed, groceries to be bought—such an endless array of mundane matters. In the midst of these, however, is the real business of living—a friendship to be formed, a marriage to be mended, a child to be encouraged, a truth to be driven home, an apology to be made, a Christian attribute to be further developed." (Neal A. Maxwell, Quote Book, 217)

CHAPTER 2

Ministering Angels Seen and Unseen

"My beloved brothers and sisters, I testify of angels, both the heavenly and the mortal kind. In doing so I am testifying that God never leaves us alone, never leaves us unaided in the challenges that we face. "[N]or will he, so long as time shall last, or the earth shall stand, or there shall be one man [or woman or child] upon the face thereof to be saved."
Elder Jeffrey R. Holland[1]

Part of *consecrating our waits* in life is being available to be an angel, or an answer to someone else's prayer. I propose that we seek the Spirit of the Lord to know how to help others through difficult times in their lives. When I had been out for three months on my mission in Peoria, Illinois, I received some devastating news that my mother had terminal ovarian cancer. It was a complex situation as I am a convert and my mother was not a member. My mother was amazing through the whole thing and showed a tremendous amount of faith!

She wanted me to stay on my mission; she told me as long as I stayed in the mission field she knew she would have God's special care.

Fast forward to just ending my sixteenth month of my mission; up to this point there had been some really difficult days where we didn't know if my mom was going to make it through the night and many tears were shed and prayers were given. I always knew I was to stay on my mission. Also, my mom always said to please not come home. Then, the miracle happened—about nine months after her diagnosis, my mother was going into remission! I felt such relief and continued on my mission.

Again, at this point, I had been out a little over 16 months, my companion, Sister Heather Rothey, and I had come home from doing a night of calling back on investigators. I received the phone call from my mom telling me that her cancer was back with a vengeance and that her doctor thought she had less than a month to live. I could hear my Mom crying on the phone; this pained me to the very core. I had tears streaming down my face, but I wouldn't let her hear me cry; I was trying to be strong for her. After calls with my home Bishop, Stake President, and my Mission President Fenton Burgess, I hung up and was physically ill from this very stressful development in my mother's health. Sister Rothey came over to me and tried to hug me, but I pulled away. I knew if I started crying, I would not be able to stop. I wanted to go to bed and not talk about anything.

I recently talked with Heather about this time and asked her what she could remember. That night as we were getting ready for bed, Sister Rothey wanted to have our usual night prayers. I didn't want to say it, because I knew if I talked I'd start to cry. Sister Rothey said the prayer…a few things we both remember…"Heavenly Father, I know I don't hold the priesthood, but I pray in the name of Jesus Christ that thou wilt bless Sister Martin and if possible let me help carry the burden she is carrying. Help her to trust me and know she can tell me all she is feeling. Help her to know she is supposed to go home at this time." She expressed our love to Him and her love for me and asked again to bless her that she could help carry my burden and make it lighter for me. During the prayer, the Spirit was so strong that I started to weep. I sobbed like a baby. I felt so much sadness, pressure, and stress. Sister Rothey held me like a baby and I cried most of the night. I think it was all of the tears I held in my whole mission. God's miracle came and she was able to carry that burden and make it lighter. *The Lord truly granted that prayer.*

In talking recently with Heather, she said she has never had that experience since; that is, to be able to truly feel and completely carry the burden of another. It was a very powerful moment that I felt the love of the Lord. This was in January of 1991.

I did return home that week. Sadly, my mother passed away two weeks later.

In his wonderful talk *Angels, Chariots and the Lord of Host,* Professor Donald W. Parry (in a BYU devotional in July 2012) eloquently said regarding angels:

> "How many angels are there? There are hosts of angels. The *Old Testament* expression 'Lord of hosts' sometimes refers to the Lord of hosts of angels. The

Bible Dictionary states: "The Lord of Sabaoth was a title of Jehovah; the hosts were the armies of Israel (1 Samuel 17:45), but also included the angelic armies of heaven." Hebrew lexicons agree with this interpretation. One prominent Hebrew lexicon states that the term *Lord of hosts* sometimes refers to "the heavenly beings" of the Lord or "the heavenly entourage" of the Lord. Another Hebrew lexicon agrees with this definition, referring to a host as an "(organized body) of angels."

"The title "Lord of hosts" is so important that it is found some 250 times in the *Old Testament*; Isaiah alone used the term about fifty times. This title, then, is a frequent reminder that the Lord has hosts of angels. How many angels belong to the Lord of hosts of angels? The singular host, by definition, refers to "a large number of people or things." The plural, *hosts,* multiplies this number. The Lord of hosts of angels refers to immense numbers."

"Other passages of scripture also indicate that there are great numbers of the Lord's angels. For example, Lehi envisioned "God sitting upon his throne, surrounded with numberless concourses of angels." (1 Nephi 1:8) Two passages of scripture—Hebrews 12:22 and *Doctrine and Covenants* 76:67—use the expression "an innumerable company of angels."

"Furthermore, John the Revelator recorded: "And I beheld, and I heard the voice of many angels round about the throne…and the number of them was ten thousand times ten thousand, and thousands of thousands." (Revelation 5:11)

"Indeed, ten thousand times ten thousand angels, which equals 100 million, symbolizes a great number. To sum up, there are numberless concourses of angels, an innumerable company of angels, and hosts of angels—all of whom are in the service of our Lord and God."[2]

I loved this and absolutely loved this talk! Having lost both of my parents fairly young; my mother in 1991 and my father in 2007, I believe they are now my guardian angels and I believe that many angels are helping us that we will never even be aware of. "I believe we need to speak of and believe in and bear testimony of the ministry of angels more than we sometimes do."[3]

More Angels Among Us

It was May of 1992, I was living with a dear friend, Katrina, who had recently joined the Church. I had been missing my mom terribly and was feeling discouraged with my life. I went to bed with pensive and heavy thoughts. For the first time in a long time, I slept very sound that night. Although I didn't see her, I truly felt like I had been comforted by my mother's spirit. I couldn't quite remember, but I had awaken feeling much lighter than the previous day. As I went into our living room, Katrina was waiting for me to share what she had experienced the night before. This is her account written in the back of my journal as a second witness (shared with her permission):

"While fast asleep one night, I awoke startled, with a feeling of spirit filling the apartment. My thoughts were clear and vivid, "There are angels in my room!" Again, later I awoke, *"There are angels definitely in my room!"* I couldn't see them nor did I know who it was. That morning I told Michelle of my experience and how great and wonderful I felt, how close I felt to the Lord's wonderful mysterious other world. She explained that her mother had visited her that night and I knew it was the truth; she had been there to console and comfort her daughter of whom I'm sure she watched over continuously. I bear testimony of the truth of this gospel and am grateful for such a marvelous experience that brought me closer to the veil." (Katrina McCloskey Troutman, 1992)

I also remember her telling me she thought someone left the light on in the hall because she could see light through the base of her door—there was no light on in the hall. Talking with Katrina recently, she said, "This was such a testimony strengthening experience as a new member in the gospel of Jesus Christ. I can never deny that angels are real and they are among us."

In the spring of 1998, I took a wonderful trip to the Holy Land with a dear friend, Cathy Larsen. It was incredible to walk where Jesus walked. We had many great experiences going all around the Sea of Galilee, Jericho, Bethlehem, the Dead Sea, etc. One of my favorite places was visiting the magnificent BYU Jerusalem Center. Pleasantly surprising was our groups visit to the Orson Hyde Memorial in Jerusalem. This is a pathway that leads from the BYU Jerusalem Center to the Garden of Gethsemane. This place was blessed by the

Apostle Orson Hyde, during the early days of the restoration of the Church in the 1800s. I walked and looked out over the city Jerusalem. I had such a peaceful feeling while walking along the Orson Hyde Memorial. It wasn't any big impression or anything; I just knew my mother's spirit was with me. It was a sweet tender mercy of the Lord. The interesting thing was later on when we were back at the bus, Cathy and I were talking about the day and I told her about my experience, Cathy said she too had felt her brother's presence (who had died two years earlier in a tragic hiking accident). Another lady on the bus had overheard us talking about this; amazed, she told us that she too had felt her deceased mother's presence there. That is a sacred place! This was such a loving reminder, as well as a testimony to me that our loved ones are with us more than we know! ☺

Many times in our lives we will have the opportunity to be angels to others. The Lord has blessed me tremendously with angelic friends, kindred friends—truly lifelong friends! I challenge each of us to call upon ministering angels daily to help us, and to be looking for opportunities to be angels to others as well! ☺

CHAPTER 3

The Miracle of Visiting and Home Teaching

"Each of us, from time to time, is mentored and has chances to mentor. In my experience, truthful and caring one-liners that occur within such nurturing relationships have a long shelf-life! You can probably recount three or four examples of how people have said something—probably a sentence or clause—and you remember it still. It moves and touches you still. Such has been the case with me."
Elder Neal A. Maxwell[4]

It was the summer of 2015, and for a few months I had been assigned to visit teach Jill. After a few attempts, I finally got through on the phone. Our first conversation didn't exactly create what you would call warm fuzzies and goose bumps! It was in July when we first talked.

Our conversation went like this: "Hi Jill, this is Michelle, your visiting teacher." There was a hesitant pause, "Oh,... (awkward pause)...Hi" from Jill. I could tell by the sound of her voice she wished she hadn't answered the phone (she might have even rolled her eyes ☺). I asked if I could come have a brief visit with her. She said, "You don't need to come, I don't even go to church anymore. You don't really need to come." I said, in the kindest voice I could, "I know I don't need to come, but I'd love to come for just five minutes to say hello and get to know you." She then replied, "Well, you don't really need to; besides, I am a school teacher and I am off for the next three weeks on a road trip with a friend, so I won't be around." I felt very directed by the Spirit to say, "Oh, that sounds fun! I'll tell you what, why don't you go on your road trip and when you get back we can take that five minutes of you telling me about yourself and your trip." With a defiant voice she said, "Oh, okay, you can just get a hold of me when I get back." After our conversation, I went to the local store and bought a few hand wipes, licorice, and just a few simple things for her road trip. I left them on her door in a little bag with a simple 'have a fun and safe trip' note.

About a month later (and after several attempts to align our schedules), we finally met. When I first went to her apartment, she invited me in with some caution. I asked her to tell me where she was from, etc. As she started telling me about herself, a girl came around the corner in the kitchen and said, "Hi I'm Sandra (name changed)" and went into their kitchen. I realized it had been close to five minutes that I had been there. I told Jill that it had been five minutes and asked if I could share a brief message before I left. I had no idea what I was going to say, since I had planned on just hearing about her road trip and about herself. She hesitantly agreed to let me share a message. Under the direction of the

Holy Ghost, I said, "Jill, ever since we talked in July I have felt strongly that Heavenly Father knows your name and speaks it often! I know Heavenly Father wants you to come back to church and I need you to tell me what my role is in helping this happen?" Jill immediately softened and shared how she had really struggled with her faith due to certain challenges that had weighed very heavy on her heart. She went on to say she just didn't have faith anymore; she said it was too hard to believe there was hope. I then told her I knew why Heavenly Father sent me to be her visiting teacher. I shared with her that I was 46 years old, never married or had children, and that there was nothing more in life that I wanted than that! I told her I didn't know why that blessing had not come into my life, but I had two choices—I could choose to despair and be discouraged (I told her I've done that and that is not a happy path), or I could choose to trust God even though I couldn't see ahead. I told her I didn't know why we must struggle with the things that we do, but God does and He does love us. I told her I now knew why God had sent me to visit teach her. I challenged her to hold onto her faith, dig deep, and not let go!

Meanwhile, Sandra—her roommate at the time—peeked around the corner and said, "I really like your message. Can I come and listen?" I said, "Sure." I soon realized Sandra wasn't a member. She asked several questions about the Church. I then told her I was a convert. They both said they'd like to know God had a plan for them and their lives. After a nice discussion I left them with a word of prayer.

I had tried to get a hold of the local missionaries' phone number that week, but life got busy and I didn't call. Then

Jill texted me saying she felt like her roommate was ready to meet with the missionaries and she should probably sit and listen in too. ☺ She then asked if I could arrange that. As you can imagine, I was so happy to oblige! Shortly after this, Jill texted me and asked me if I would come to her house as she and Sandra were both sick and were wanting priesthood blessings. These young missionaries (maybe 18 or 19 years of age) were filled with the Spirit as they laid their hands on both their heads and gave them beautiful blessings. They blessed Jill that she would know that God loved her and knew her by name (the very thing I was prompted to say to her) and also that although it had been a long time since she walked with the Savior, He loved her and desired her to come back to Him. As they blessed Sandra they told her they were true messengers of Jesus Christ and blessed her that if she would listen to the things they had to teach her they would teach her truths that would lead her back to Christ and help her know who she really is.

A long story short—Sandra and Jill were taught the discussions by the missionaries and Sandra was baptized about six weeks later into The Church of Jesus Christ of Latter-Day Saints. Jill started meeting with the Branch President and was preparing to come back to the temple. She started changing her social life decisions by associating with others who were uplifting around her.

About three months after I first met with them, I taught a lesson in Relief Society from the life teachings of President Ezra Taft Benson on helping others come back into the fold. I wrote every sister's name on a piece of paper and put their names in alphabetical order on chairs. We then had all the sisters come in and find their name and sit in the chair with their name on it. The room had many empty chairs. We discussed how the sisters felt about the empty chairs, etc. There was a fantastic quote from the manual that talked about not giving up on each other and being persistent in helping those come back into the fold. Jill raised her hand and said, "Can I make a comment?" Jill then shared with our Relief Society sisters how she and I met and how her visiting teacher wouldn't give up on her and wouldn't take no for an answer. She was emotional as she talked about the changes she was making with the help from the Spirit and priesthood keys. Many in the class were very touched with her sensitive sharing. One year after I met Jill, I attended the Salt Lake Temple with her and her mother! ☺

I share this story that we may realize that we *never* know when God will use us to help someone else! We never know when *He* needs us to bring *His* smile to others! Up to this time I had been struggling with fitting into this new small branch I had been attending. I had really started to wonder if God had forgotten me. I had been feeling very discouraged that God didn't need me or that He didn't have any purpose for me. I'm grateful for my testimony of visiting teaching. "The work of reactivation is done a soul at a time, quietly and with dignity…and if some bristle a bit, then let us learn how to pat a porcupine." (Neal A. Maxwell, *Ensign*, May 1982, 37)

A few days after my Dad passed away from cancer (2007), I was sitting on the couch at home feeling truly paralyzed by my grief—having now lost both of my parents. My dear friend, Angie Lawrence, knocked at my door. I remember she asked what she could do to serve me. I was in such a state

I couldn't think of anything. I did, however, have a basket full of laundry and couldn't get myself to do it. It was too much, it required too much energy—I was literally unable to function. Angie grabbed that basket and did my laundry and a few other things during that visit. Although she wasn't my visiting teacher at the time, we were serving in a Relief Society presidency together. I will forever be grateful for her kindness and selfless gesture! It was such a great example of extending the Lord's love to others, by being an earthly angel!

I learned a long time ago that no matter how hard life gets, you *always* go to church and we should always visit teach or home teach! Satan wants nothing more than to hold us back from fulfilling the measure of our creation and being where Heavenly Father needs us. If we do those two things: always go to church and fulfill our home and visiting teaching assignments, we will have the blessing of our baptismal covenants. We can't afford to not have His Spirit to be with us! We never know when the Lord needs *us* to bring the smile of Jesus to others!

One observation I have is that so many of us are extremely busy—I know; I live a busy life too! But it amazes me that some sisters will find time to watch *The Bachelor* on TV or in my case *Dancing with the Stars* and yet, they can't find a night to visit teach. Same with our priesthood holders who can find time to watch the NBA finals or some crime show, yet—they can't find time to home teach.

Home Teaching: While in a singles ward, I was blessed to have two stellar and dedicated home teachers! I want to share with you about Dave McCallister and Drew Johnson. Drew has mild intellectual disabilities and really wanted to home teach. Dave was so committed to home teaching and to helping Drew have a great experience that he would go to Drew's home and read through the message with him and Dave would highlight the parts that Drew wanted to share. Monthly, they came faithfully to my home and every other month Drew would hand me the message and point to the highlighted areas that he wanted to share.

Another sweet memory I have with these two loyal home teachers was when I was sick and needed a blessing. I called Dave and he said he'd be right over. He picked up Drew and then came to my home. Drew was pretty nervous and Dave basically walked him through every single word as he anointed before Dave gave the blessing. After the blessing, Drew had tears in his eyes and humbly said, "Thank you for allowing me to use my priesthood."

CHAPTER 4

Trust the Lord and Call Upon Angels

"Could we with ink the ocean fill? Was the whole Earth of parchment made? And every single stick a quill and every man a scribe by trade? To write the love of God above would drain the ocean dry, nor could the whole upon the scroll—be spread from sky to sky."[5]

I testify that God lives, that He knows each of us by name and speaks our names often! I love this beautiful saying above of how *He* feels about us! I want to start out by sharing one of my favorite scriptures in the *Old Testament*. Shadrach, Meshach, and Abednego will not deny the God of Israel and are about to face possible death and be cast into the furnace of fire:

> If it be so, our God whom we serve is able to deliver us from the burning fiery furnace, and he will deliver us out of thine hand, O king.

…that we will not serve thy gods, nor worship the golden image which thou hast set up.

Then was Nebuchadnezzar full of fury…commanded that they should heat the furnace one seven times more than it was wont to be heated.

And he commanded the most mighty men that were in his army to bind Shadrach, Meshach, and Abednego, and to cast them into the burning fiery furnace.

Then these men were bound in their coats, their hosen, and their hats, and their other garments, and were cast into the midst of the burning fiery furnace.

Therefore because the king's commandment was urgent, and the furnace exceeding hot, the flames of the fire slew those men that took up Shadrach, Meshach, and Abednego.

And these three men, Shadrach, Meshach, and Abednego, fell down bound into the midst of the burning fiery furnace.

Then Nebuchadnezzar the king was astonished… and spake, and said unto his counsellors, Did not we cast three men bound into the midst of the fire? They answered and said unto the king, True, O king.

He answered and said, Lo, I see four men loose, walking in the midst of the fire, and they have no hurt; and the form of the fourth is like the Son of God.

Then Nebuchadnezzar came…and spake, and said, Shadrach, Meshach, and Abednego, ye servants of the most high God, come forth, and come hither. Then Shadrach, Meshach, and Abednego, came forth of the midst of the fire.

And the princes, governors, and captains, and the king's counsellors, being gathered together, saw these men, upon whose bodies the fire had no power, nor was an hair of their head singed, neither were their coats changed, nor the smell of fire had passed on them. (Daniel 3:16-27)

I think most of us have enjoyed sitting around a wonderful campfire up in beautiful canyons or at the beach. Usually, when we come back down the canyon, or from the beach, the smell of fire is in your hair, skin, your clothes, etc. The smell doesn't go away until we shower. But here, Shadrach, Meshach, and Abednego had not even a hair on their head singed and the smell of fire had passed by them! I testify that God the Father and His Son Jesus Christ will *also stand with us* through any furnace that is placed before us! Satan has a big lie out there that we are buying into—that God has abandoned us, forgotten us or we are here alone to make it through this mortality! That is absolutely not true! *God has not, CANNOT, and WILL NOT abandon us! They—God the Father and Jesus Christ—love us, know us by name and speak our names often! That is God's truth! I want to share this truth with you.*

In his famous talk, *All These Things Shall Give Thee Experience*, Elder Neal A. Maxwell stated, "The thermostat on the furnace of affliction will not have been set too high for us—though clearly we may think so at the time. Our God is a refining God who has been *tempering soul-steel for a very long time.* He knows when the right edge has been put upon our excellence and also when there is more in us than we have yet given. One day we will praise God for taking us near to our limits—as He did His Only Begotten in Gethsemane and Calvary."

"We will also see that our lives have been fully and fairly measured. In retrospect, we will even see that our most trying years here will often have been our best years, producing *large tree rings on our soul,* Gethsemanes of growth!"[6]

I want to share with you two of the many times THEY— God the Father and His Son Jesus Christ—have stood with me through a difficult trial or otherwise, a furnace of affliction. Referring back to the news of my mom's cancer diagnosis while on my mission. I had been out about three months. It was also the week before Christmas where, for a few weeks, my heart had been heavy with thoughts about home and I didn't know why. On this particular day, we had been blessed with about a foot and half of snow in Illinois. As my companion and I were walking in the door of our apartment, the phone was ringing. I immediately felt sick to my stomach and knew that it was for me. My companion answered the phone, looked at me and said, "Sister Martin, they asked for Michelle." I took the phone and said hello. I then heard my sister Mattye state gravely, "You may want to sit down Michelle." I asked, "Is it Mom?" She asked, "How did you know?" I answered, "I don't know. I just know something is wrong!" She proceeded to tell me that my mother had ovarian cancer that had spread to her lungs and the prognosis was not good. They were saying she had about 4-6 months to live and that my mother was scheduled for a radical hysterectomy and chemotherapy treatments in the upcoming weeks. She gave me a few more details and we agreed we'd talk in a few days again on Christmas.

When I hung up the phone, my companion, Sister Stock came over and wrapped her arms around me. Emotionally, I felt as if I'd been hit with a golf club! I went into the bathroom and was sick. I then told my companion I needed to be alone and went into the bedroom. I fell on the bed and cried and cried—I thought my heart would literally break. After what felt like hours later, my companion came into the room, put her arms around me and said, "Sister Martin, we are going to make it through this together with the Savior's help." She hugged me one more time and then left the room.

I then slipped off the bed straight to my knees and prayed and prayed like I had never done before. I poured my soul out to Heavenly Father, pleading for Him to please help me! After a time, I remember looking up, and on the wall above my bed was a photo of Christ in the Garden of Gethsemane. Eventually, I felt as if His loving arms were wrapped around me, letting me know that no matter what happened, I would be okay because of His Atonement. He truly was bearing my grief and carrying my sorrows (Isaiah 53:4). I wasn't sure how, but I knew with my Savior and Heavenly Father's help I somehow would make it through this time.

Fast forward to 2010: I had a very unhealthy—actually toxic—situation at work that I needed to remove myself from. After prayer, fasting, going to the temple, and ultimately a blessing I received from my Bishop, I knew I needed to leave my job. This was not logical at all, as I did not have another job lined up. Nonetheless, this was the clear answer from the Lord. The morning I was to give my notice, I was praying and started to cry—feeling a bit like a Red Sea was ahead of me. I could barely focus on anything, so I thought that I would read one scripture for my scripture study that morning. I chose to read a favorite scripture from a Relief Society Newsletter that a sister had shared—so I opened to *Doctrine and Covenants* 6:23 and it read, "Did I not speak peace to your mind concerning the matter? What greater witness can you have than from God?" That day I went in and gave my two-week notice. During this time, I was blessed to find temporary work as a dental hygienist and as a seminary teacher. I did whatever I could to make ends meet until I found a job. About four months later, I was getting pretty discouraged and starting to feel a sense of panic. I went to one of my best friend's houses and her husband gave me a blessing. Now this worthy priesthood holder had given me several blessings before, however, he had never reviewed scriptures with me before a blessing. This time Blake said right before the blessing, "Michelle, I feel impressed to review a scripture with you before the blessing." We all went and sat down and he opened his scriptures to (you can probably guess) *Doctrine and Covenants* 6:23 and he read, "Did I not speak peace to your mind concerning the matter? What greater witness can you have than from God?" I started to get a little weepy. Was God in the details of my life?—ABSOLUTELY! Is HE in the details of my life today?—the answer is YES! Is HE in the details of your life? YES!!!

President Uchtdorf lovingly reminded us, "Though we are incomplete, God loves us completely. Though we are imperfect, He loves us perfectly. Though we may feel lost and without compass, God's love encompasses us completely.... He loves every one of us, even those who are flawed, rejected, awkward, sorrowful, or broken."[7]

I also want to testify that we can call upon ministering angels to help us! Although I have never seen them, I know both my parents who have passed on, have helped me from time to time. In Elder Jeffrey R. Holland's great talk *The Ministry of Angels,* he stated:

"I ask everyone within the sound of my voice to take heart, be filled with faith, and remember the Lord has said He would fight our battles, our children's battles, and the battles of our children's children. And what do we do to merit such a defense? We are to search diligently, pray always, and be believing. Then all things shall work together for our good, if we walk uprightly and remember the covenant wherewith we have covenanted. The latter days are not a time to fear and tremble. They are a time to be believing and remember our covenants."

"My beloved brothers and sisters, I testify of angels, both the heavenly and the mortal kind. In doing so I am testifying that God never leaves us alone, never leaves us unaided in the challenges that we face. "Nor will he, so long as time shall last, or the earth shall stand, or there shall be one man or woman or child upon the face thereof to be saved." On occasions, global or personal, we may feel we are distanced from God, shut out from heaven, lost, alone in dark and dreary places. Often enough that distress can be of our own making, but even then the Father of us all is watching and assisting. And always there are those angels who come and go all around us, seen and unseen, known and unknown, mortal and immortal."[8]

Adversity will come to all of us in this mortal institution! I promise this, if you will dig deep, stay the course, keep praying, keep going to the temple, keep searching the word of God, and DON'T give up your faith! Hold on!!! Do as President Uchtdorf said, "Doubt your doubt, before you doubt your faith."[9] Reach out to others!!! HE will stand with you through *any* furnace of affliction! We MUST TRUST IN THE LORD through our adversities! He will reach our reaching! The Lord said, "I will go before your face. I will be on your right hand and on your left, and my Spirit shall be in your hearts, and mine angels round about you, to bear you up." (*Doctrine and Covenants* 84:88) I know this is true, for God is a Perfect God and a God of Truth and HE CANNOT LIE!!!

Side note: This chapter was a talk I gave in an evening Stake Conference—it's been modified to be a part of this book. A month before I gave this talk, I was invited by some wonderful friends to enjoy a beautiful private concert at their home. There was lovely, heavenly music played with a piano, cello, and violins. During the concert, the song "If You Could Hie To Kolob" was played. While listening to this song, I noticed they had a lovely piece of art on their wall that depicted a lady with many angels above her with their hands on her head; in my mind, they were giving her a heavenly blessing.

A couple of weeks later, I was diagnosed with pneumonia and was very sick. I had a few particularly hard nights where

I wasn't sleeping at all and had trouble breathing. I even had a night where I coughed so hard I vomited while in bed—I was miserable! Trying to calm and comfort myself, I started listening to a CD of that same song "If You Could Hie To Kolob" from the same friends who had the concert in their home. I decided to pray for ministering angels to come that night and give me a heavenly blessing. Next thing I knew, I was asleep and slept all night long; not once did I cough that night. I knew the prayer had been answered. ☺

Fast forward three weeks later when I spoke in the Stake Conference evening session. They asked me to speak for 15 minutes. I had written a talk and timed it—it was exactly 10 minutes. I didn't want to just throw a scripture in to fill the time. I read more scriptures, listened to more conference talks, and listened to more music. After listening to the song, "If You Could Hie to Kolob," one more time and remembering my sweet experience, I decided to add the blessing of being able to call upon ministering angels to my talk. The beautiful miracle I experienced was at the evening session of Stake Conference. There were three speakers, a musical number, me and then our Stake President. Guess what the musical number happened to be? Yes, you guessed it…"If You Could Hie to Kolob." The Lord was truly in the details!

CHAPTER 5

Appreciate Liberty!

Our freedom was won long ago by men young and men gray.
Their courage was strong, they fought for their faith,
And they were quick with no delay!
Next time you vote or kneel to God to offer your soul to pray,
Remember those heroes of long ago,
That paved freedom's way.

I wrote these words years ago while visiting Lexington and Concord in Massachusetts. I was touched as I stepped back into time and took the journey from Lexington to Concord. I learned that there were many families where three generations fought on the same day; sons, fathers, and grandfathers all fought in this war that paved freedom's way!

Another great way we can *consecrate our waits* in life is to live in appreciation of the many freedoms we have here in America—freedom of religion, freedom of speech, freedom to receive an education, to vote, and countless others! The

U.S. Constitution—the document our founding fathers wrote to secure those liberties—has been called a 'Heavenly Banner' by the prophet Joseph Smith.[10]

President Ezra Taft Benson stated in his famous 1986 talk on the Constitution, "Look back in retrospect on almost six thousand years of human history. Freedom's moments have been infrequent and exceptional. We must appreciate that we live in one of history's most exceptional moments—in a nation and a time of unprecedented freedom. Freedom as we know it has been experienced by perhaps less than one percent of the human family!"[11] Just an interesting side note, three years after this talk was given the Berlin Wall came down overnight!

In my work, I sit on the State of Utah's Refugee Health Advisory Board. Some of these refugees have been victims of torture and violence. Some of these refugee mothers want to help their children learn to read and write in America, but they, themselves, are not literate in their own language because they did not have the right to be educated. I realize that especially as a woman in America, I am extremely privileged. There are some countries where women can't even show their faces in public. I am grateful for my education and the fact that I have a library card in my purse that I can use anytime I want to check out any book I would like.

My job gives me the great privilege to provide dental screenings and oral health education to refugees. While meeting with a group of refugees in an English as a Second Language (ESL) class, we gave each participant a toothbrush, floss, and toothpaste. One lady said she would be happy to now share this toothbrush with her family. I then kindly taught that she would really want to use her own and they should each have their own. I then learned from her that while they spent several years in a refugee camp, they shared a single toothbrush and the same washcloth with her whole family. I silently thanked Heavenly Father for my many blessings I enjoy every day and take for granted.

In 2002, while on the streets in Ho Chi Minh City, Vietnam, I saw a little girl that looked like she was 3 or 4 years old who tried to sell me gum and cigarettes. I could see on the side street a man waiting for her to bring him the money. My heart ached for this little girl. What was her future? Let us expand our hearts with gratitude for truly ALL that we have!

In April of 2016, I spoke at the National Oral Health conference in Cincinnati, Ohio. I fell in love with this city as I walked along the Ohio River and saw the lush green grass and trees that line it. While there, I visited the National Underground Railroad Freedom Center. I was truly touched by this place and it made an imprint on my heart! It's main purpose and tribute is stated in the museum, it is, to 'abolish human enslavement and secure freedom for all people.' I was inspired by tributes to the lives of so many great people from the past, like Harriet Tubman, Frederick Douglas, Harriet Beecher Stowe and countless others who were instrumental in freeing many slaves during the 1800s.

Two sisters I had not heard of were Sarah and Angelina Grimke. They were two Caucasian women from the south that were proactive abolitionists who showed great courage during the vile, horrible time of slavery. Both were witnesses as children to the cruelty of slavery: they watched slaves labor to over exertion in corn and cotton fields. They both secretively taught slaves how to read, wrote letters and pamphlets against slavery, sat with slaves in church services, and later on in life were voices for the women's suffrage movement. I was grateful for these women who were a voice for those who did not have a voice. For more information on these two sisters read online at: www.nps.gov.[12]

A few other things that were somber to see and learn about (information taken from the Underground Railroad Freedom Center):

- There are more slaves today worldwide than were seized from Africa in four centuries of the trans-Atlantic slave trade. Human trafficking and illegal drug trafficking is global reach, millions of dollars is made each year from this horror—and destroys many lives.[13]

- The chocolate industry is worth an estimated $110 billion a year, and yet it's key commodity is grown by some of the poorest children in the world, who have been taken into slave labor.

- Unfortunately, enslavement and human trafficking is not of the past—it is the fastest-growing international crime.

- Millions of girls around the world face barriers to education.

- There are countries where there is literally no freedom at all—such as North Korea—males and females are equally oppressed, there is no freedom of speech, religion, education, or choice of any kind; something most of us in America have been blessed with for years.

- There are more than 43 million displaced refugees throughout the world.

- At the Underground Railroad Freedom Center, they also advertised a new documentary that puts a spotlight on child trafficking called *The Abolitionists*—ideas are shared of how you can help support those stopping child trafficking.

- Harriet Tubman made 13 trips to free over 70 other slaves. That is some serious courage, especially when there was such a bounty on her head!

When I think of freedom, I also think of moral agency—what an amazing gift! Elder Richard G. Scott said, "The right of moral agency is so important to our Father in Heaven that he was willing to lose one-third of his spirit children so that it would be preserved." (BYU Speech, 1999) How grateful I am for Jesus Christ for his role in the Plan of Salvation to make agency possible. I recently read a book called *Escape from Camp 14: One Man's Remarkable Odyssey from North Korea to Freedom*. This book is about a 23-year-old man who was born in a political camp and basically lived with zero free agency. One of the things that kept him alive was the fact that he knew how to capture rats and eat them. He was beaten or disciplined almost daily. Three generations of his family had been in these camps and he never knew why.

Living in this choice land of America comes with great privilege, but it also comes with great responsibilities. I'd like to suggest four things we can do to show appreciation for our liberties, for the blood that is still being spilt for us every day so our freedoms might be preserved.

One—Pray for the Leaders of Our Nation and ALL Nations

This includes putting our nations leader's names on the temple prayer rolls and including them in our fasting and prayers, that they may have and use discernment from God. Many of God's children are being brought to America either as immigrants or refugees, but they are coming! We have a great opportunity to love them and serve them. Many have come from very difficult circumstances!

> Wherefore, I, Lehi, prophesy according to the workings of the Spirit which is in me, that there shall none come into this land save they shall be brought by the hand of the Lord.
> Wherefore, this land is consecrated unto him whom he shall bring. And if it so be that they shall serve him according to the commandments which he hath given, it shall be a land of liberty unto them; wherefore, they shall never be brought down into captivity; if so, it shall be because of iniquity; for if iniquity shall abound cursed shall be the land for their sakes, but unto the righteous it shall be blessed forever. (2 Nephi 1:6-7)

Two—Pray for Our Brothers and Sisters

Pray for those that are living in oppressed lands that have zero freedom—that hearts will be softened and miracles can bring them to the knowledge of God's love. We have witnessed this miracle over and over again in many countries. We can learn about refugees and see if there are any living in our local areas and if there is something we can do to help them.

For instance, volunteering to help them learn English, or asking a resettlement agency how you can help (www.rescue.org). The Church of Jesus Christ of Latter-Day Saints also has a new program to help and mentor refugees called *I Was A Stranger* (https://www.lds.org/refugees). For more information about refugees, see Elder Patrick Kearon's talk *Refuge from the Storm*, in the May 2016 *Ensign*. This photo shows Kaylee Crossley, one of my interns, and myself teaching refugees at the LDS Humanitarian Center about oral hygiene.

Three—Read the *Book of Mormon* and Appreciate this Great Gift

Great sacrifices were made that we could have this unblemished record and account of the life of the Savior. There is no way the First Vision and all of the marvels of the Restoration could happen in a country that did not have freedom of religion! This includes the wonderful miracle of the *Book of Mormon* coming forth to us!

I remember the first time I read the *Book of Mormon* all the way through. I had read intermittently the first year after I was baptized, but I had not read it cover to cover. I realized a month before my one-year anniversary as a member of the Church that I had not ever read it all the way through. I decided I would read it in 30 days. I took the total number of pages in the book and divided that by 30 and read that many pages every day for a month. It was such a powerful experience. I felt the Spirit of Christ more in my life than I ever had at that point! It really was a turning point in my testimony of the Church and of understanding more of Jesus Christ.

I also learned that using the *Book of Mormon* on my mission was one of the most powerful teaching tools and ways to bring others to Christ! I witnessed there was definitely a different spirit of conversion for those who read the *Book of Mormon* and those who did not!

President Ezra Taft Benson said, "I bless you with increased understanding of the *Book of Mormon*. I promise you that from this moment forward, if we will daily sup from its pages and abide by its precepts, God will pour out upon each child of Zion and the Church a blessing hitherto unknown—and we will plead to the Lord that He will begin to lift the condemnation—the scourge and judgment. Of this I bear solemn witness."

President Benson continues on with, "Our beloved brother, President Marion G. Romney,...who knows of himself of the power that resides in this book, testified of the blessings that can come into the lives of those who will read and study the *Book of Mormon*." He said, "I feel certain that if, in our homes, parents will read from the *Book of Mormon* prayerfully and regularly, both by themselves and with their children, the spirit of that great book will come to permeate our homes and all who dwell therein. The spirit of reverence will increase; mutual respect and consideration for each other will grow. The spirit of contention will depart. Parents will counsel their children in greater love and wisdom. Children will be more responsive and submissive to the counsel of their parents. Righteousness will increase. *Faith, hope, and charity— the pure love of Christ—will abound in our homes and lives, bringing in their wake peace, joy, and happiness.*"[14]

President Ezra Taft Benson said, "These promises— increased love and harmony in the home, greater respect between parent and child, increased spirituality and righteousness—are not idle promises, but exactly what the Prophet Joseph Smith meant when he said the *Book of Mormon* will help us draw nearer to God."[15]

Four—We Must Remain Purposeful

And, behold, there cometh one of the rulers of the synagogue, Jairus by name; and when he saw him, he fell at his feet,

And besought him greatly, saying, My little daughter lieth at the point of death: *I pray thee*, come and lay thy hands on her, that she may be healed; and she shall live.

And *Jesus* went with him; and much people followed him, and thronged him.

And a certain woman, which had an issue of blood twelve years,

And had suffered many things of many physicians, and had spent all that she had, and was nothing bettered, but rather grew worse,

When she had heard of Jesus, came in the press behind, and touched his garment.

For she said, If I may touch but his clothes, I shall be whole.

And straightway the fountain of her blood was dried up; and she felt in *her* body that she was healed of that plague.

And Jesus, immediately knowing in himself that virtue had gone out of him, turned him about in the press, and said, Who touched my clothes?

And his disciples said unto him, Thou seest the multitude thronging thee, and sayest thou, Who touched me? *(I can see them saying Master, look around, there are a lot of people here, many are touching you.)*

And he looked round about to see her that had done this thing.

But the woman fearing and trembling, knowing what was done in her, came and fell down before him, and told him all the truth.

And he said unto her, Daughter, thy faith hath made thee whole; go in peace, and be whole of thy plague. (Mark 5: 22-34)

Here we see the Savior was very busy; with being whisked away to heal Jarius's daughter, with many people following him, and as the scripture says, *thronging* him. He was doing very important work and healing many along the way. Amidst this busy schedule, a faithful woman comes along that has struggled with this illness and heavy burden for 12 years. She has such faith in the Savior that she could be healed just by touching his garment. I am sure this was something He was very used to by now, and since He was dealing with a life and death situation it would be understandable if he continued swiftly onto Jarius's home. Yet, He did NOT! The entire incident where he stops to acknowledge this woman's faith probably took about five minutes. Despite His busy schedule, He persisted in purposefulness by acknowledging her faith and put her mind at ease to go in peace. In a worldwide devotional for young adults, Randall L. Ridd said:

> "So many times we get distracted when we should have acted. Distractions rob you of time that could have been invested in doing good." (January 2015)

Think of our crazy schedules; between family, kids, visiting teaching, home teaching, scripture reading, work, school, volunteering, church callings, going to the temple, everyday errands, trying to get in exercise, etc., do we take time to be purposeful? Do we take a moment to ask the clerk at the store or bank how their day is going? Do we respond to inspiration to call a friend or family member? Let us never forget that living in a free nation comes with great privilege, but with that comes great responsibility. Let us remain purposeful as we live in this land of privilege and liberty; seek to be where God needs us to be, consecrating our time, and blessing who we can, where we can…even amid our crazy schedules!

To close the thought of appreciating our liberties, I want to give a list of things we can do while *consecrating our waits.* I already talked of four ways to show more appreciation of our freedoms. Here are a few things we can do to be proactive in sustaining our own and helping others embrace liberty:

- Read this link that gives 15 ways you can fight human trafficking. See http://m.state.gov/mc42492.htm.

- Be a registered and educated voter and then get out and VOTE!

- Show gratitude to our troops and show support to their families back home.

- Read about our forefathers and learn about our American History.

- See www.ourrescue.org to learn how you can help those who support rescuing children from sex trafficking.

CHAPTER 6

Testify to Others of Whose We Are

"Every month the First Presidency and the Twelve meet with all the General Authorities in the temple. They bear testimony and they tell each other how they love one another just like all of you.... Do you think that you can go three, and six, and nine, and twelve months without bearing your testimony and still keep its full value?"
Président Spencer W. Kimball[16]

When I was 17 years old, I was searching to find truth. I attended many different churches with several different friends. I also had been to various LDS church dances, early morning seminary, and a few church meetings, but I was not a member of the Church yet. It was a Sunday afternoon and I was home with my Mom. I don't remember why, but I had disappointed my mom, and I was feeling very down. My friend, Karen, called me to see if I wanted to go to a "fireside" with her. I truly thought maybe we would be outdoors by a campfire and that there may even be s'mores served. ☺ I attended the fireside with her, her sister Lynette, and several other friends that night. I remember as the speaker came to the pulpit he started by saying, "Who am I," and he continued by repeating the question, "Who am I?"

I thought to myself, *I am a horrible person. My mom is mad at me…*while he continued "I am a son, I am a father, I am an uncle, I am an American citizen, I am (whatever his occupation was)," and then he paused and it became very quiet and he said, "I…am a child of God."

He looked into the audience and looked at me, *almost as though he looked through me* and said, "You are a child of God." And then he looked elsewhere and said, "You are a child of God." I was not familiar with the Spirit and what it felt like, but I got a lump in my throat and all of a sudden I started to cry. I was a little embarrassed and didn't know what to think, so I left the meeting.

I walked down the hall, found a phone, and called my sister and her husband, who are members of the Church. I asked them if I could talk to the missionaries that night. My sister made a few phone calls and I ended up meeting with them that night and was baptized three weeks later. The Spirit truly witnessed to me that I was a child of God.[17]

Spencer W. Kimball has taught us: "As a vital link in the conversion process, we should bear our testimonies that the gospel is true; our testimonies may well be the spark that ignites the conversion process. Consequently, we have a double responsibility: we must testify of the things we know, feel, and have felt, and we must live so the Holy Ghost can be with us and convey our words in power to heart of the investigator." (Spencer W. Kimball, "It Becometh Every Man,"*Ensign*, 1977)

In December of 2002, I was preparing for a humanitarian trip to Saigon, Vietnam. It was the day before Christmas and I was to fly out the next day. I was feeling anxious about the trip and having a long flight over an ocean. I asked for a priesthood blessing from a member in our bishopric. Some of the things I remember that were said were: I was blessed with safety and that I was going to a land that would one day have a temple. Also, that the gospel would be brought to the people of Vietnam, little by little at first, through humanitarian efforts. As the blessing continued, I was told that I would serve pure and noble spirits who were not here to be tested, but to teach love…*(Wow, I thought!).* So, needless to say, I was comforted and on my way to the beautiful country of Vietnam.

While there, we had many amazing experiences working in orphanages and helping build a kindergarten in a village located in a city called Hue, which is in the central area of Vietnam. I remember the day before we were about to leave Vietnam to come home, I thought about the blessing and thought that I sure did meet amazing humble people, but was sad if I missed the lesson on love. It was on our way to the airport that we stopped by a handicapped orphanage in Saigon. We saw infants and children living in a way I hope to never see again. It was horrific what we saw! We were taken rather quickly through the orphanage. There was a room where infants were kept. They were alone, and smell of urine was palatable. Most of the babies were in boxed crates that were saturated with urine. The Buddhist monk (a woman with a shaved head) wanted to keep us moving in the orphanage, as if she knew how horrified we were.

An interesting side note: There was a Buddhist temple that was next to the orphanage that had fine gold and a lot of money tied into it, obviously not a cent went to the orphanage.

Everyone had left the room with the Buddhist monk. I stayed behind and saw a little infant boy, maybe five months old. He had an underdeveloped hand and was staring at the

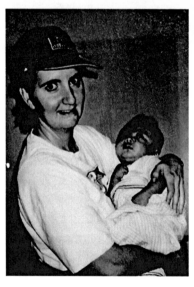

wall. He had open sores on his bottom from his rash and had an open lesion on his inner thighs. We were told not to touch any of the children with open wounds, so we would not pick up any infections. I found a blanket and picked up this *pure and noble spirit*. He was staring off and you could tell was suffering with attachment loss—seldom being held and rarely if at all changed and cleaned. I snuggled him in my arms and softly started to sing in his ear "I Am a Child of God." As I was singing, this little noble spirit slowly moved his head toward me and gazed into my eyes. We had a spirit to spirit communication. Basically, the Lord wanted me to know through this little guy that I was a child of God— *this infant was teaching me who I really was!!!* It was a very powerful and sacred moment.

It was probably 3-4 minutes later that someone from our American group said, "There she is." I looked up and a flash of a camera went off. Someone had taken my picture with this baby. As I looked down to him, he had gone back to staring at nothing; I knew our communication was over. The beautiful blessing had been fulfilled—I had been among pure and noble spirits; but specifically this one I knew was not here on earth to be tested, but was here to teach love.

A few Christmases ago, I was in a very dark, lonely place of despair; this can happen if I don't stand guard at the door of my mind with negative thoughts. I have a hard time opening up to others when I am struggling. I was blessed this day to receive a phone call from one of my ministering angel friends Cara; she called to tell me she was thinking of me and how much she knew that the Lord knew me. I don't remember all that she said, but I do remember the Spirit and love of the Lord that I felt that night—light permeated my soul! Thank goodness for ministering angel friends! ☺

In his family memoir *Faith of My Fathers*, John McCain shares his personal hardship and tragedy of being a prisoner of war in Vietnam. He shares moments of being captured, breaking both arms and a leg, continuous physical torture, spending much of his time in solitary confinement with horrible neglect during his five and a half years into captivity from 1967 to 1973. He discloses one of his lowest times of being detained in a very small box for solitary confinement. In his words he shared, "Once I was thrown into another cell after a long and difficult interrogation. I discovered scratched into one of the cell's walls the creed, I believe in God, the Father Almighty. There, standing witness of God's presence in a remote, concealed place, recalled to my faith by a stronger, better man, I felt God's love and care more vividly that I would have felt it had I been safe among a pious congregation in the most magnificent cathedral."[18]

While watching a news broadcast on television one night, I heard John McCain talk about this gruesome, yet bitter-sweet account. He said those few scratched words on the wall restored his faith and will to survive.

> "If I can just be one more voice to say that God lives and that this is His work, I will be satisfied."[19]

The man who spoke at the fireside long ago about how he was a child of God, along with my ministering angel friend and the man in captivity that wrote those power-ful words inside a dark imprisoned boxed wall that helped John McCain feel hope; all of these people may never know how much their testimonies helped and impacted others. I believe this is true for all of us. We will never know the power that lies in sharing what we know to be true and the potential of being exactly where God needs us! I know God lives, I know Jesus Christ is the Savior of the world and His atonement is real. I know Joseph Smith is a prophet and he truly saw what he said he saw; the *Book of Mormon* is the word of God. There have been many times that I have been struggling or feeling low and I am spiritually invigorated when I bear my testimony.

Sharing our testimonies can truly bless the lives of others to extents we will never know. I also know that bearing your testimony can strengthen us tremendously as well.

The Prophet Joseph Smith testified, "And now, after the many testimonies which have been given of him, this is the testimony, last of all, which we give of him: That he lives!

"For we saw him, even on the right hand of God; and we heard the voice bearing record that he is the Only Begotten of the Father." (*Doctrine and Covenants* 76:22-23)

Every time I read these verses I feel the Holy Ghost witness of their truth! A closing challenge to this chapter is to bear your testimony *today!* Bear it to your family, spouse, roommate, write it in your journal, bear it in church—keep it simple and based on Jesus Christ! Now there is nothing wrong with bearing a 'travelmony' or sharing stories in testimony meetings, but the core strength in these meetings comes from bearing a pure testimony of God the Father and His wonderful plan of happiness with the Savior Jesus Christ being our advocate with the Father. *He lives, all glory to His name.* He lives! He is ever watchful. They know us by name! Take time to share this knowledge often and you will be strengthened, as well as being able to edify others!

CHAPTER 7

Trials as Mercies in Disguise

"For the faithful, our finest hours are sometimes during or just following our darkest hours."
Elder Neal A. Maxwell[20]

Frequently I listen to Christian radio stations. There is a song that I love by a talented singer, Laura Story, called "Blessings." In this song there are lyrics that ask, "What if trials in this life are your mercies in disguise?" Although the Apostle Paul said he gloried in tribulation, I don't believe I would ever say that! However, I must admit looking back through the death of my parents and a few other difficult dark times in my life, that these were also tender mercies in disguise, even though they were such agonizing emotional times.

In the Fall of 2012, I woke up with a terrible backache on my left side. It hurt all day and I had a little 2-inch rash on my hip. I thought I had hurt it at the gym, but I was so busy at work with different speaking assignments that I hadn't taken the time to go get this rash and pain checked out. The next night, I asked a neighbor-friend to take me to the emergency room (ER) because I thought I was passing a kidney stone or something. I was in excruciating pain! After several hours in the dang ER, I was told I had shingles. What?? Shingles?? "Are you sure?" I asked the physician, "Isn't that what 80 year olds get?" She reassured me that I truly had shingles and had the classic rash. She sent me home with a prescription and told me to rest.

I had two speaking engagements at work that next week where I was the keynote speaker; I wasn't sure how I could not go. So, I probably did not do the smartest thing. Even though I filled and used the prescription, I continued on with my busy work schedule. All this did was prolong the illness. I had back aches, burning fire on my side, insanely intense headaches and fatigue; basically, I have never been so physically miserable in my life. The thought of a semi running me over almost sounded inviting. With all that said, I must admit it was through this 7-week difficult illness that I was strengthened with heavenly help and experienced some tender mercies!

Let me share a few of them: During this time, I was teaching gospel doctrine and had a substitute cover one of my lessons. I then realized the next lesson I was to teach was 3 Nephi 17 (a beautiful chapter in the *Book of Mormon* where Jesus Christ and ministering angels bless many children). There was no way I was going to miss teaching that lesson. While reading and preparing the lesson all week I felt like the veil was thin at my home. Basically, moving from my bed to the restroom or to the kitchen two times a day was about all the energy I had.

During this week, my friend went and picked up a book that I had requested at the library. As mentioned before it was the book on CD; *Escape from Camp 14: One Man's Remarkable Odyssey from North Korea to Freedom.* I listened to it all day in bed on one of the days that I was home. Again, this was a true story based on a young man who was raised in a political camp in North Korea with absolutely *no freedom.* He ends up miraculously defecting to China and then eventually into South Korea. The atrocities that he and all those in his camp endured everyday made me disgusted and also sad.

This chapter in the *Book of Mormon,* was on my mind since I was going to somehow teach it on that following Sunday. It was then that I had an epiphany. Basically, Christ had come after a horrible genocide of those who believed in Him and He wept, prayed for them, loved them, blessed them, and so much more. The scriptures say words can't be uttered what was said and spoken on that day. If Christ knew all that they went through in 3 Nephi, *I knew HE completely knew all the pain and suffering of those in North Korea. His Atonement covers it all! And if HE knew their pain and suffering, that can only mean that HE knew mine, and loved me and wanted to comfort me in my own time of suffering.* I know it sounds very simple, but it was so powerful! I testify that God does know all of our joys and all of our sufferings. He is completely aware of us!

Another tender mercy at this time was a blessing of healing I received from my friend's husband and their son Keltson. Keltson had just received his mission call and the Melchizedek Priesthood. So this was Keltson's first experience giving a blessing. They brought the most amazing spirit to my home; it was such a tender mercy during this illness.

"I testify that the tender mercies of the Lord are real and that they do not occur randomly or merely by coincidence. Often the Lord's timing of HIS tender mercies helps us to both discern and acknowledge them."[21]

GOD IS AWARE OF US
AND IS IN THE DETAILS OF OUR LIVES!!

More Tender Mercies

In the Spring of 2010, I had the great privilege to travel to the beautiful city of Cuzco, Peru for a three-day conference with a non-profit organization called *Reach Out and Learn*. We traveled to provide continuing education for medical and dental professionals on various topics. I researched and prepared a presentation on Oral Cancer and the Human Papilloma Virus. The rest of the volunteers and I stayed in Cuzco the day we presented and helped out with the conference. On the days we didn't speak, we were taken to a very remote village about an hour away from Cuzco at a very high elevation. These people lived off the land and spoke their tribal language.

I was scheduled to speak the second day of the conference; consequently, the first day I was able to join those going to the village. We planned to paint their little school, pass out soccer balls, and have lots of fun little trinkets and games for the children. We traveled about eight miles up a windy, narrow, and treacherous road. Some of us were struggling with bad headaches because of the altitude. We were told this road is traveled by a car about once a week; we were on a bus carrying all of us and our equipment. Looking over the edge around each switchback was making me a bit queasy and nervous. I have to admit; I was saying a few silent prayers along the way. The mountain terrain that surrounded us was majestic with several hues of lush greens; it was absolutely stunning! The sunshine was glowing and we were blessed with deep blue skies. Later on, I was to realize what a blessing that sunshine was for us!

When we were one mile from the village there was a problem with our bus and it completely broke down. We all streamed out of the bus basking in the beauty that surrounded us and began taking lots of photos. Then we each started realizing the gravity of our situation. The village was still about a mile up this dirt road and we were approaching 13,000 feet in altitude with lower oxygen levels. Knowing that this dirt road only sees about one car a week, we decided to say a prayer that help would come. We then witnessed a *true miracle*—within minutes; not *one*, but *two* cars were driving up the hill!

During the previous few weeks, these wonderful people of this village had been devastated by torrential rains, and were threatened by mud slides and losing their homes. One of the cars was actually a truck. This governmental truck had come to discuss with the villagers the damage done to the village. The other was a car coming to help the villagers also. There were 18 adults in our group and several teenagers with us. Those teenagers and a few of us walked along a trail that led to the village while the rest of the adults fit in these two vehicles with our supplies and rode up to the village.

When we arrived, we were greeted by these beautiful indigenous families. We immediately got set up and started painting their school. The wonderful teenagers that were with us played soccer, jumped rope, and played other games with the children. They were so full of joy; it was lovely to watch them! When we finally took a lunch break, we played games with the children and watched them with total bliss as they experienced blowing bubbles for the first time. ☺ We also had fun playing hokey pokey with them; they loved it when we got to the part of turning ourselves around.

Now for the other part of the miracle: the windy, narrow, and treacherous road was a dirt road. We were so grateful for fabulous weather. Had it rained, that dirt road would have been muddy, wet, and non-drivable. This was a tender mercy!

The next day that we went to the village, we helped rebuild a greenhouse that had been partially destroyed. Their main source of food is corn and potatoes. Someone from our group had brought a few seeds to see if there was a way we could help them grow other sources of nutrition. There were many homes closer to the edge of the mountain that were threatened to slide off due to the torrential rains. We saw government tents where some families were living temporarily until they could rebuild their homes because several of the homes had already slid off. We were simply trying, in a small way, help these beautiful people whose homes were being threatened.

In his beautiful talk on tender mercies, Elder David A. Bednar said, "I testify that the tender mercies of the Lord are available to all of us and that the Redeemer of Israel is eager to bestow such gifts upon us."[22]

Recently, I witnessed another wonderful tender mercy and miracle. I had received a text from my downstairs neighbor letting me know that water was coming from my condo upstairs. As I got home, I discovered that my air conditioning (AC) unit had a clogged PVC pipe and was leaking water all around my AC unit and into my neighbor's condo below me. The last time I had someone address a problem with my AC, I felt like I had been taken advantage of and I believe they were dishonest. I immediately prayed that I would be guided on what to do. I called a dear friend, Jonathan, who works for an emergency clean up company. He was so kind and came right over. After a trip to Home Depot, he fixed part of the problem and brought over two professional, heavy-duty-24-hour fans that dry out floors and carpets that have been flooded. He also sprayed my wet areas so they wouldn't get moldy.

The next day, we realized that there was water leaking still. I went to be by myself and specifically prayed out loud that Heavenly Father would send ministering angels to help me know who I should talk to, that they could diagnose this, fix the problem, and not break the bank for me. The next night Jonathan came again and became frustrated, as he knew there was a blockage, but couldn't find where it was. He told me I would need to call an AC specialist to fix the problem.

As the phone was in my hand to call the number of the AC specialist, my Relief Society president called me to discuss someone I visit taught. In the course of our conversation, I told her what was happening with my AC. She then said, "Michelle, call Bill. That is what he does for a living." Bill was our Elders Quorum president; I called him, he came over within an hour, and diagnosed the problem in three minutes! Yes, three minutes! Within an hour and half the problem was fixed and it cost me a total of $15 dollars in parts!! What a tender mercy! I was so grateful for this wonderful miracle! God is truly in the details of our lives. He cares about us. As we draw upon the powers of heaven through prayer and call upon ministering angels, we will continue to see tender mercies in our lives!

One last tender mercy story I want to share is not mine, but that of my Stake President and his lovely wife Kendra. They shared with me about the tender mercies that occurred in their lives during the terminal illness of their son, Bryce. Some of this information was given at the Sandy Midvalley Stake Conference in September 2015 and some was given in an interview with Ken and Kendra Moss. While Bryce was diagnosed with post-transplant lymphoproliferative disorder cancer, their family experienced many tender mercies in disguise that witnessed God is truly in the details of our lives and in all circumstances.

After the death of their son, who died at age 26, Ken and Kendra Moss made a list of 32 tender mercies that happened during his illness. With their permission, I will share a few of them:

- In 1985, after Bryce had his first kidney transplant and it failed, Ken was given three job opportunities which helped double their income (compensatory blessings) and helped pay for all their medical bills. This was a very stressful time!

- The Lord preserved Bryce's life in October and January. Bryce was not prepared to meet the Lord then because he had a few unresolved things he needed to work out with his Bishop. He was able to do this and his Bishop felt that he was prepared to meet the Savior.

- The Lord blessed Bryce to have Jerica (his girl-friend) and her family come into his life so that even though the last four months were some of the most difficult in terms of pain for Bryce, they were also the happiest. We know that Jerica was the angel that Bryce had been promised in numerous priesthood blessings would come into his life! With our limited understanding, we don't know why they were not able to be sealed, but we have great faith in the compensatory blessings He promises!

- The Lord preserved Bryce's life for six weeks and allowed us the wonderful blessing of serving Bryce, which we greatly cherish. We were able to be with him and he was able to know someone was there, even when he was confused; we tried to help alleviate his pain, turn him to be comfortable, and help him brush his teeth. Kendra (Bryce's mom) shared that she was able to sing to him and rubbed his feet and back to help calm him). Some told us that he could have passed away the first few days after he went into liver failure, while others have spent their last few weeks on a ventilator. We were blessed to have Bryce rebound and be off of a ventilator the last three weeks.

- Other extended family members were able to help tend children. This allowed his sisters, Heidi and Alisha, to say good-bye to Bryce in a timely manner. (This was not the original plan!)

- Bryce was purified with the refiners' fire during this very difficult time, always expressing gratitude and a thumbs up to everyone. He could walk around the hospital after his coma—he was so determined to get better! The Lord helped him and 'reached his reaching' physically.

- Ken's work was close to the hospital so he could take his computer and work at the hospital. His work allowed him to be very flexible! ☺

- A miracle happened when Bryce turned 26; he was still covered under their insurance until he passed, which helped us tremendously financially. God intervened with this detail…in fact, God was in the details of all of it!

- Our family grew closer through this adversity.
- We received many kindnesses from numerous friends and family.
- Many meals and visits were given to us (Ken was the Stake President during this time).

Ken and Kendra both received the gift of greater empathy for others because of their suffering. During such a difficult time, they were able to see God in the details and the tender mercies in disguise. I have been so strengthened by this couple's faith during such an arduous time and being able to see the Lord's hand amidst severe adversity! Regarding compensatory blessings, Elder Joseph B. Wirthlin said:

"The Lord compensates the faithful for every loss. That which is taken away from those who love the Lord will be added unto them in His own way. While it may not come at the time we desire, the faithful will know that every tear today will eventually be returned a hundredfold with tears of rejoicing and gratitude."[23]

Think of a difficult time in your life. I know it can be hard to go there emotionally. Think back and if you look with God's understanding and teaching, you will see there were miracles along the way. I challenge you to remember the tender mercies and miracles in life even when, *and especially when,* life is hard! WRITE THEM DOWN!! ☺ Also, I challenge you to believe that *compensatory blessings will come!*

In the last example shared, this family was experiencing much 'long suffering' as they were *waiting* for their son to pass beyond the veil into the eternities. Seeing God's tender mercies in their lives while they waited through this time is a perfect example of *consecrating our waits* in life! I love and appreciate the example of Ken and Kendra Moss!

CHAPTER 8

Defy
Your Limits

"I can do hard things."
Elaine S. Dalton[24]

While *consecrating my waits* in life, I like to challenge myself in positive ways. I want to grow spiritually, mentally, physically, and however I can to be what the Lord needs me to be. In January 2016, I made my typical New Year's goals; one of which was to hike Mount Timpanogos in Utah. After starting out the year with a miserable case of pneumonia, I wondered how the rest of my year would be.

I started hiking every Wednesday and Saturday in May in preparation for this goal and was grateful for a couple of wonderful friends that hiked with me. The week of the Mount Timpanogos hike I prayed that I would have ministering angels, and my family members that had passed on, help me up to the summit! On the day of the hike, we left our homes at 3:40 a.m. to hit the trail just after 4:10 a.m. We realized at over a mile and a half into the hike that we were on the wrong trail. I started to feel very discouraged and didn't know if I could hike 16 miles plus 3.7 more miles that day. We headed back to the parking lot so we could take the right trail. As my mental state was a little gloomy, I heard the thought clearly in my head, *"I survived Vietnam, you can do this."* I knew it was my Uncle Roger who had passed away four years earlier from lung cancer. I felt strengthened and knew I would have help that day!

While hiking, we saw more than two dozen mountain goats, many beautiful wildflowers, majestic mountain peaks, lush landscapes for miles, and bright blue skies—I knew God had truly created all of this for us to enjoy in our lives!

It was a very strenuous hike! When we finally reached the saddle, the view was breathtaking; we could see miles and miles in all different directions. It was a beautiful clear day. I must admit, I was super worn-out and didn't know if I could go another step. The summit was one more mile up a very steep, narrow, and rocky terrain. One of my best friends, Camille Kennard, was with me and she was such an amazing cheerleader all along the way! She kept saying, "You can do hard things; you got this!" Her Dad helped me through all the really steep areas. I was so grateful for their love and support! ☺

I struggled with nausea from altitude sickness for the last bit to the summit. Finally, I made it to the top of the summit and it was the most magnificent and stunning view! I felt such an accomplishment. We had a rough start with being delayed, but we did it! I ran out of water with 5 miles left before getting back to the trailhead, and the last 4-5 miles were the worst miles of my life. My feet ached so badly, I almost cried when I finally reached the parking lot. This day I had truly pushed beyond my physical limits. Camille, who is a social worker and also a life coach, has a sign on her vision board where her goals are; it says, *"Live to defy your limits."*

While on a trip to the Polochic Valley in Guatemala, I was specifically there to do basic oral hygiene education and provide local anesthesia for villagers that were needing to see the dentist for abscessed teeth. Many of these teeth needed extracting or had infections or were rotted out (sadly, there were many). Each day we set up a clinic in a different village and drove from village to village in the back of a cattle car. One particular day, many of our medical and dental people were struggling with traveler's diarrhea. Consequently, we were very low with staff and should have called it a day, but there were so many people waiting to see us that we decided to stay and see those that we could.

In this area there were two different languages spoken; Spanish and Q'eqchi. We needed two translators at all times: one that translated English to Spanish and then one to translate from Spanish to Q'eqchi. I personally never met someone that was fluent in all three. We also had no electricity or running water. We brought in bottled water to use for sterilization. There were more than 30 families waiting outside to be seen just for dental alone.

Our other hygienist was helping in another village that day, so I was by myself screening and triaging. We had a young father of four come in with a significant abscess and some swelling in his face. This was NOT a good sign, and we were not in a position to give him optimal care with certain antibiotics. So I numbed him on the side of his face where the infection was, which provided immediate relief. I then walked over to our medical clinic to see if they had a stronger antibiotic to give him.

While on my way there, several moms grabbed at me asking me with their faces to "please see their children." One lady was pointing at her 3-year-old signaling for me to look in her mouth. Meanwhile, she had an infant on her hip that had something moving under the skin of its eyelid. I gently clasped her hand and signaled for her to follow me. She kept putting my hands toward her 3-year-old. When I got to the medical clinic (which also had a long line), I asked if they had a stronger antibiotic and the attending nurse gave me a "what the heck is that?" look about the infant's eye. We found out later that the child had a parasite under its eyelid.

Eventually, I started to make my way back to the dental clinic. While walking back, many mothers were again giving me begging faces of "please look at my child," "please see my child." It was super overwhelming. To top it all off, we had an English/Spanish translator but we did not have a translator that spoke Spanish and Q'eqchi, which was vital so that the young father could understand how to take his antibiotic regimen.

All of a sudden, I couldn't take the stress anymore. I said to my friend Adam, who was holding a flashlight for me to see while I was administering local anesthesia, "I need just a minute." I went into a corner in the dark (again, we had no running water or electricity with very limited provisions). There was also nowhere else to go as many families were

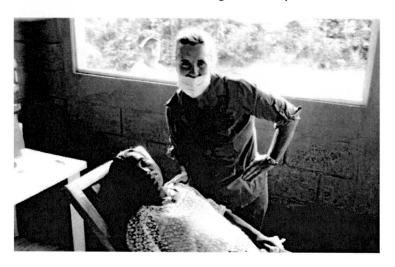

right outside the door and the one window that we had. I couldn't hold back the tears and started to cry, then prayed, "Heavenly Father, this is too much. I am way in over my head here. I don't speak their language. I don't even know this man's name. Please help him understand that he needs to take this medicine everyday like he's supposed to. Please, Father help me. I am way over my head here!" I had a quick breakdown of tears and suddenly I felt super calm with a clear mind and thought, *Michelle, you are more than enough. I know you don't know this language or his name, but I DO.*

Go back over there, (I was literally 2 feet away from the crowd) I know Q'eqchi and I know each of these people by name. I got this and I got you! I then squared my shoulders, took a deep breath, turned around and said, "Okay, I am ready." Adam, who was helping me, said, "What just happened?" I said, "I'll tell you later." He said he could tell by my face something happened. ☺ About five minutes later, a villager walked in and asked if we needed a translator that spoke Q'eqchi. He

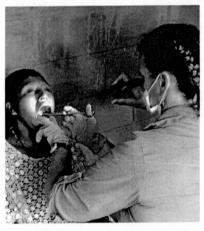

spoke this language along with Spanish and ended up translating for us and telling this young father all that he needed to do for post treatment after his extraction.

We truly witnessed a tender mercy and miracle! I will always be grateful for Heavenly Father's friendly reminder to me that *HE knows ALL of us by name and is aware of ALL our needs!* We can truly do hard things with His help!

When life gets hard and the *waiting* is excruciating in life—challenge yourself! Whether it is a spiritual challenge like reading *Jesus the Christ*, learning a new language, taking an art or tai chi class, or hiking a mountain—push yourself! You can do hard things! Ask for ministering angels to help you! *Live to defy your limits!*

CHAPTER 9

Sling and a Stone

"You need not fear if you have the slingshot of truth in your hands. You have been counseled and taught and advised. You have the stones of virtue and honor and integrity to use against these enemies who would like to conquer you. When they challenge you, you can hit them "between the eyes," to use a figurative expression. You can triumph over them by disciplining yourself to avoid them."
President Gordon B. Hinckley[25]

One of the great stories of courage from the *Old Testament* is the story of David and Goliath. I believe there are many applications from this story for our own lessons of life—it is an account I need to read more often! This story is found in 1 Samuel 17. First of all, we discover that Goliath of Gath (the Giant) is six cubits and a span in height. After doing a little research, I found that this measurement indicates that Goliath was 9 feet 9-inches tall (*LDS Old Testament Student*

Manual, Genesis–2 Samuel, 278). To me, facing a 9-feet 9-inch-tall giant would have been very intimidating, but not David, he was full of courage and faith. He takes a moment to remember the Lord's help and deliverance in earlier circumstances. This is a great message to us when we are full of doubt, fear, or despair!

We all, at one time or another, will face our Goliaths. Think about your life; what is yours? Is it a wayward child or a wayward spouse? Is it a marriage that is distant and falling apart? Is it some form of an addiction? Is it pornography, time in front of the computer with social media or prescription drugs? Is it unemployment, being under-employed, singlehood, loneliness, or an unexpected tragedy in your family? Is it death, divorce, depression, illness, or infertility? Is it time management and finding balance? The list goes on and on. Many other things could be our Goliaths.

So how can David's example help us as we face our own Goliaths in life?

We read in 1 Samuel 17: 37: "David said, moreover, The Lord that delivered me out of the paw of the lion, and out of the paw of the bear, he will deliver me out of the hand of this Philistine. And Saul said unto David, Go, and the Lord be with thee."

Again, we read how David is remembering the Lord's hand and deliverance at an earlier time. This is a friendly reminder to me that as we have difficult things in front of us we need to *remember* earlier times when the Lord has helped us or delivered us or given other miracles that have happened in our lives. We've all had them! We must *remember* that if

He helped us through a hard time before, He will help us through a hard time now! The day of miracles has NOT ceased! As we continue on, we read the whole incident of David against the Philistine Goliath:

And when the Philistine looked about, and saw David, he disdained him: for he was but a youth, and ruddy, and of a fair countenance. *(Do we have times when others may scorn us or look down on us? Or tell us we don't measure up?)*

And the Philistine said unto David, Am I a dog, that thou comest to me with staves? And the Philistine cursed David by his gods.

And the Philistine said to David, Come to me, and I will give thy flesh unto the fowls of the air, and to the beasts of the field. *(Sounds similar to some modern day bullying.)*

Then said David to the Philistine, Thou comest to me with a sword, and with a spear, and with a shield: but I come to thee in the name of the Lord of hosts, the God of the armies of Israel, whom thou hast defied.

This day will the Lord deliver thee into mine hand; and I will smite thee, and take thine head from thee; and I will give the carcasses of the host of the Philistines this day unto the fowls of the air, and to the wild beasts of the earth; that all the earth may know that there is a God in Israel. *(Remember he is looking at a giant that is 9 feet 9-inches-tall standing in front of him. ☺)*

And all this assembly shall know that the Lord saveth not with sword and spear: for the battle is the Lord's, and he will give you into our hands.

And it came to pass, when the Philistine arose, and came and drew nigh to meet David, that David hasted, and ran toward the army to meet the Philistine.

And David put his hand in his bag, and took thence a stone, and slang it, and smote the Philistine in his forehead, that the stone sunk into his forehead; and he fell upon his face to the earth. *(Just an interesting side note: we read earlier in verse 40 that he chose five stones and had them with him in his bag. He only needed one, nonetheless, he was prepared for whatever he needed to do.)*

So David prevailed over the Philistine with a sling and with a stone, and smote the Philistine, and slew him; but there was no sword in the hand of David.

Therefore David ran, and stood upon the Philistine, and took his sword, and drew it out of the sheath thereof, and slew him, and cut off his head therewith. And when the Philistines saw their champion was dead, they fled. (1 Samuel 17: 42-51)

I'd like to share with you one of the Goliaths in life that I have had to face. Now, before I start, I want to make it clear that I believe I am truly blessed with a good life. With that said, I will share with you that personally one of my biggest challenges and questions that I just don't have an answer for is the waiting to marry and share my life with someone. For a very long time, I listened to Satan's lies—telling me it was because I did something wrong, or wasn't pretty enough, or missed an opportunity somewhere. Year after year, I have watched more friends marry, have children, and now they are sending those kids to college and on missions. Of course, I am so happy for my friends when the great events of life (marriage, children, grandchildren, etc.) happens for them. I must admit though, that it is hard to understand why the Lord hasn't seen to provide me with this blessing.

Yet, more recently in the last few years, I have come to understand that God does love me. He knows me and He truly wants the best for me! I used to jokingly say that I'm working on plan B, then plan C, and eventually I'd gotten to plan S. However, *I now know* that I am living the Lord's plan A for me. Just because these blessings haven't been realized doesn't mean that He loves me less or wants less for me! It just means that His plan and purpose for my life is different than I expected. I still believe that I will be married in this life! I can choose to doubt and despair (and trust me I have—not fun), or I can choose, as David did, to remember the Lord's hand in my life in earlier times and know that He is here for me now!

Having lost both my parents, I also struggle with wanting to belong to a family and have someone to share my life with. I have a brother and sister in the Portland, Oregon area who I love very much, but we don't live close to each other. This can make holidays very lonely. I have been blessed with great friends, but I long for a family of my own. Most of the time, I feel at peace and live a very purposeful and abundant life. However, there are moments, usually holidays, that can cut so deep to the core of my heart that I think it could literally bleed. I truly want to *consecrate this waiting time* to God's purposes and helping others!

Back to David, he had in his pocket five smooth stones, but only used one. He put them in his shepherd's bag and had in his hand his sling. This was how he was preparing himself to face the Philistine, Goliath. What are the stones and slings in our lives? These are the measure of our preparations. Although there are many to prepare, I'd like to share five smooth stones, and the one sling of my own, that have truly blessed my life!

First Stone—Gratitude

It takes effort to exercise gratitude and have an optimistic approach to life. Yet the Lord truly blesses us, and His tender mercies should not go unnoticed or unappreciated. The *Book of Mormon* prophet Moroni reminds us of the importance of gratitude and encourages us to "remember how merciful the Lord hath been unto the children of men, from the creation of Adam even down until the time that ye shall receive these things, and ponder it in your hearts."[26]

We also read in *Doctrine and Covenants* 59:21: "And in nothing doth man offend God, or against none is his wrath kindled, save those who confess not his hand in all things, and obey not his commandments."

One suggestion and challenge I'd like to give is something I learned from my mother. My amazing mother always had thank you cards on hand. She always sent thank you notes and Christmas cards. I believe correspondence of gratitude expands the soul! I know for myself, when I have unexpectedly received a letter of gratitude it warms my heart. Years ago I decided to have a box of thank you notes at work and in my church bag. Having had many opportunities to speak professionally and teach at church, I know preparation can take a long time so I try to be more aware of people and the little things they do and express appreciation. I know I could still improve at this and I want to work at cultivating this attribute of gratitude.

Second Stone—Personal Prayer

As mentioned before, John McCain was a prisoner of war in Vietnam and suffered from many brutal beatings. He later wrote this about prayer, "I was finding that prayer helped. It wasn't a question of asking for superhuman strength or for God to strike the North Vietnamese dead. It was asking for moral and physical courage, for guidance and wisdom to do the right thing. I asked for comfort when I was in pain, and sometimes I received relief. I was sustained in many times of trial."[27]

The following is a tender story of personal prayer, shared by Joann Montesinos who served her mission in Warsaw, Poland. This is a great example of being specific in our prayers! In her own words, and with her permission, this is her account:

"I wanted to preface this experience by saying that this isn't a 'typical' missionary story about prayer that we're all used to hearing. It's not the kind of story in which my companion and I prayed to find the perfect family, were guided by the Spirit to a certain house, taught the whole family, and they were all baptized. Though it's not one of those stories, it still was a profound experience that taught me a great deal."

"I had been on my mission for a little less than a year. At the time, the branch in the area I was in had about five or six members total, two of which were active. The rest absolutely hated us because we tried going over to their houses every other day. All day, every day, more than in any other city I served in, we were on the streets trying to stop people and talk to them."

"It was the middle of my second transfer, and the lack of outward success was taking its toll on me. I started having a hard time finding the motivation to even bring myself to go out anymore, and Sister Wendel, my companion, was going through the same struggles. For a few days I found myself praying something like, "Father in Heaven, I know nobody here knows who I am, but this city is full of tourists who come in and out, can't someone just recognize me as a missionary and say hi?" After a few days I decided I was going to find a different way for Sister Wendel and I to get motivated again because what I had been asking for was silly."

"A couple of days later, Sister Wendel and I were really struggling trying to talk to people on the streets. We couldn't find any motivation at all to be doing what we were doing, so we decided to change our plans a bit. We thought it would be better to take the tram back home, and go through the area book to make some phone calls and try to set up a few appointments that way. So we started making our way to a tram stop, one that we didn't normally go to but it was the closest to where we were."

"The city we were working in has a tourist tram that goes around the city and takes tourists around to the major sights. The tram-stop Sister Wendel and I were walking to, is where the tram tour ends. As Sister Wendel and I were walking towards this stop, a large group of tourists were getting off the tram. We stepped to the side to let them pass, and from the back of the crowd we see a man cutting through the group, coming towards us. He stopped right in front of us and simply said, "Hello sisters, where are you from?" It took everything I had to answer his question without crying. We were only able to talk to him for a few seconds because he had to keep up with his group, but the impact this brother had on a couple of struggling sister missionaries in Poland is one that I will forever be grateful for."

"Sister Wendel and I learned a lot that day about God's love for his children. It became very clear to us that God cares about every aspect of our lives, even to the point that he will answer seemingly silly prayers."

A while back, I was challenged to keep a prayer journal. It has been a very powerful blessing in my life! I am so easily distracted that I find, sometimes, while praying that I will start to think of my "to do" list at work. Or if I took the garbage out? Or shut the window? Or if I called that person at work? Or I start to think of different conversations during the day; my thoughts go on and on. Consequently, it's very distracting and limits me from really feeling the Spirit of the Lord and focusing on what He would have me learn from Him.

Writing down and articulating a prayer on paper, like a letter to Heavenly Father where I can pour out all of my concerns, express gratitude, and share other things on my mind helps me to focus. I will read scriptures for a few minutes and listen to some gentle hymns by my favorite LDS artists like Steven Sharp Nelson and Marshall McDonald to help set the tone and invite the Spirit. Then I will turn the page in this journal and continue to say a silent prayer for Heavenly Father's answer, putting pen on the paper and listening to revelation and inspiration that comes. It has been extremely powerful, and it has been such a beautiful experience as I have received God's truths pertaining to my life and how He feels about me.

I also wanted to share a personal experience I had with personal prayer and fasting. This is an entry from my journal:

Monday, January 8, 2008: Since last Thursday night, I have had excruciating pain from my bone spur (in my right shoulder) from repetitive motions at work (doing dental hygiene). I've been down to working two days a week as the spur has caused more pain. This week I worked three days straight of hygiene and it has just about sent me over the edge.

The last few weeks I have needed to take Ibuprofen very frequently to stay on top of the pain. I had to wake up in the middle of the night to eat food, so I wouldn't be taking the medication on an empty stomach. Saturday, all day, I was in pain. Saturday night, as I was going to start my fast for Sunday, I asked Heavenly Father if he would help me to be able to fast. I told him I really wanted to fast, but knew I couldn't if the pain from my bone spur remained.

That night as I went to bed, I didn't take any Ibuprofen at all. I said, "I won't take it if you help the pain go away." The last two previous nights from this I was awakened every three to four hours to eat and take this medication. I was so grateful to have NO pain all day Sunday. I received a blessing Sunday at church by Dave and Rob. Since Saturday night I have only taken one 600 milligrams of Ibuprofen, it was earlier today after dressing and doing dishes. I know Heavenly Father answered this prayer.

Recently I traveled to Chicago for work. Before I left, I offered a prayer, like I usually do in the morning; this time, however, I asked for ministering angels to watch over me and protect me from my house all the way to the hotel door. I made it to the airport, flew to Chicago, and took the train into town. My hotel was only four blocks from my stop. When I got off the train, I was looking on my Google Map app on my phone to find out which way to go. I had a shady man approach me and ask if he could help me find my way. I felt I should be cautious. He followed me all the way to my hotel. When we were halfway there, I thanked him for his kindness and said I could make it from there (of course, in a nice-toned voice). He started yelling at me on the street, telling me I was a racist, and that I didn't belong in Chicago and a few other colorful things. I started to panic a little. Then…I remembered my prayer; I had prayed for ministering angels to watch over me all the way to the hotel door. I knew I wasn't alone! I kept walking—this man kept following me. When we got to the hotel he asked me for money for taking me there. He said I could go to an ATM machine to pay him. I quickly went indoors and after checking in my room—a bit freaked out—I said a prayer of thanks for ministering angels that watched over me and kept me safe. I am grateful for prayer!

Third Stone—Temple Attendance

About five years ago, our Stake President challenged our stake to attend the temple once a week. At first, I thought there was no way I could do it. I made a promise to the Lord that I would try and accept this challenge. For almost five years I went to the temple every week except for occasional times where I was out of town. I have been strengthened and empowered by my temple covenants!

"Temples are designed not only to endow and to seal us but also to refine us."[28]

In 2008, a year after my father's passing, I had the great opportunity to have my father's temple work done and then seal my parents together, and then I was sealed to my parents. What a cherished memory! I desire so much to always be worthy to enter the House of the Lord! I desire to stay worthy to claim my temple sealing to my parents! ☺

President Hunter stated: "To have the temple indeed be a symbol unto us, we must desire it to be so. We must live worthy to enter the temple. We must keep the commandments of our Lord. If we can pattern our life after the Master, and take His teaching and example as the supreme pattern for our own, we will not find it difficult to be temple worthy, to be consistent and loyal in every walk of life, for we will be committed to a single, sacred standard of conduct and belief.

Whether at home or in the marketplace, whether at school or long after school is behind us, whether we are acting totally alone or in concert with a host of other people, our course will be clear and our standards will be obvious."[29]

I love that this quote states that *our course will be clear* as we attend the temple. What a beautiful promise! I don't know about you, but having more clarity in life sounds like a great blessing for attending the temple.

We receive personal blessings as we attend the temple. In *Teachings of Presidents of the Church*, Howard W. Hunter references this profound thought by Elder John A. Widtsoe:

> "Temple work...gives a wonderful opportunity for keeping alive our spiritual knowledge and strength....The mighty perspective of eternity is unraveled before us in the holy temples; ...*Then I see more clearly my place amidst the things of the universe, my place among the purposes of God;* I am better able to place myself where I belong, ...to separate and to organize the common, ordinary duties of my life so that the little things shall not oppress me or take away my vision of the greater things that God has given us. (Conference Report, Apr. 1922, 97–98)."[30]

I added the italics in that last quote. I absolutely love that he says "see more clearly my place and my purposes of God." I love the thought that if we want to understand more of our purpose in this life and how we can best fulfill the measure of our creations, we need to attend the temple and receive Heavenly Father's special instructions and love for us! ☺

Fourth Stone—Service to Others

Service to others helps me qualify more fully for the Holy Ghost! ☺ One of the great blessings of my job is being around colleagues and associates in the community that give so much of their time and their compassion in the helping of others. I work with many dental hygienists that volunteer an abundant amount of time to helping under-served populations. I also work with other health professionals, dentists, pediatricians, physician assistants, and many others that significantly give of their time and skills to bless the lives of others. They are endowed with goodness as they give back to the community they live in. They might not know it, but I believe they are "armed with spiritual life slings." ☺

One of my favorite responsibilities of my job (and frankly a sacred privilege), is overseeing the dental screenings during the Healthy Athletes Clinic at the Fall and Summer Special Olympics. Nothing warms my heart more than seeing these athletes come in with their medals on. I love to work with dental hygiene students as well as dental students, and oversee them volunteering at these events.

While in Orlando, Florida at a training for the Special Olympics, specific for Clinic Directors, I had a tender mercy. Our group was running the dental screenings and in the midst of screening hundreds of athletes, I had a very clear impression and knew all those who I was screening were Heavenly Father's special children. These athletes were so innocent and pure. It is such a sacred privilege to work with these athletes with special healthcare needs. We have fun as they come in with all their medals and smiles. I feel very strongly that if dental students and dental hygiene students work with this wonderful population while in school, they will be likely to see them in their practices when they get out of school. At the beginning of each shift, some of my student volunteers are a little nervous to do dental screenings as sometimes it can be challenging working on adults and children with intellectual disabilities. However, by the end of their shifts, they are high-fiving and hugging the athletes and smiling and congratulating them on their races. It is priceless to see this change in just a few hours.

One of my regular clinical volunteers (and now my Co-Clinical Dental Director of the Special Smiles Dental Screenings at the Special Olympics) is Kathy Harris. She is a dental hygienist and such an example of selfless service that I have witnessed at these events. Kathy has jumped in to help whenever I have been in a pinch. One time when I had a dental screener fall through at the last minute, Kathy dropped what she was doing and came in an instant. She was there early, stayed late, and helped me out tremendously. The athletes love her! ☺

There are several other services provided for the athletes (vision tests, podiatrist evaluations, wellness checkups, hearing checks, etc.). Each of these different clinics have up to 35 volunteers helping over a two-day period. All of these volunteers come on their own time and dime and love working with the athletes. If you want to be armed with God's love and power, serve those who otherwise couldn't help themselves. This is so powerful! I'm always impressed with the selfless service that so many of our volunteers render!

Frequently in my job, I provide oral health education and preventative care to Migrant Head Starts, Native Americans,

Long Term Care Facilities, Refugee Health Fairs and so many more collaborations and events. I witness volunteer after volunteer who come from all walks of life to donate their time to give back to the communities they live in. It is such a sacred privilege to witness this weekly in my life!

My dear friend, Camille Kennard, was serving in her stake as the Camp Director one summer. While at camp, the Stake President's two-year-old daughter unexpectedly passed away in a tragic accident. In Camille's words, this is what happened:

"In September of 2015 I was called to be the Stake Camp Director for our stake young women's camp that next summer. This was a huge calling and a lot of work. I had just started my business and felt overwhelmed by more demands on my time, but I accepted the call and went to work. Although I felt inadequate with organizing, making crafts, and camp certification, I knew that camp should be a spiritual experience. I began praying daily that the young women would have a spiritual and life changing experience at camp."

"The first week of June came and camp began that Monday. Tuesday night, after our overnight hike with the 4th year girls, we came back to camp and were told that our Stake President's 2-year-old daughter, Susie, had been found unconscious in their outdoor pool. She was transported to Primary Children's Hospital and was in intensive care. This was difficult news for all of us, but especially for the young women who had often babysat for the family and knew Susie very well. The girls began praying immediately for Susie's recovery and for the family. The oldest son, who found her in the pool, was a friend of many of these young women. The next morning, those in the Stake President's ward would not leave their cabin. They were immobilized with grief. I went to speak with them and they shared feelings, worries, and concerns about the family. We spoke about faith and the miracles that can happen through prayer. One of the youngest girls, a Beehive, said she had been praying for Susie that she would 'be fine and be able to go on in life.' Our camp became 'sacred' ground as all the young women were focused on faith to heal Susie and to help this wonderful family through such a difficult time."

"The next morning, we found out that Susie had passed away with her family surrounding her. This was a spiritual and sad moment. We asked a priesthood leader if he would say a prayer for the family and to heal our broken hearts. We were elevated to a higher plain as we knelt together with nearly 60 young women and their leaders pouring our hearts out to God to comfort and bless this dear family that we love so much. The spirit of the camp was angelic and the young women could feel the love of the Lord poured out upon us."

"Later that day, we had an activity about building our 'spiritual muscles' and I bore my testimony that I knew that sometimes bad things happen to good people, but that the Lord loved this dear family and that he would comfort them. I said that sometimes we go through hard things to refine us and to help us understand the Savior's atonement more deeply. We also discussed the comfort we have in knowing there is life after death. I challenged the young women to write in their journals the feelings they had at camp during the week as they combined their faith in behalf of someone else. We had truly felt the Savior's love as He reached out to us. During this most difficult time, we had an amazing spiritual camp experience. Susie's life impacted and blessed so many. Later that week during our testimony meeting, many of the young women were able to testify of the love of God and of how they felt the Spirit and their testimonies had been strengthened at camp. The young Beehive from our Stake President's ward stood up and said she felt her prayers were not answered until she realized that Susie really was 'fine' and she was able to 'go on' because she was in Heavenly Father's presence again and this knowledge gave her a lot of peace. The Lord had blessed the young women to have an experience they will never forget that built unity, love, and testimony. We had experienced a strengthening of our spiritual muscles."

As Camille served the Lord and these lovely daughters of God, she was truly armed with God's power!

Fifth Stone—Seek the Spirit

The ultimate stone to have in my life is to live worthy of the Holy Ghost—to actively invite the Holy Ghost to be with me and guide me daily! To specifically pray for the gift of discernment to be where the Lord needs us! There have been times where I have forgotten to specifically call upon the Holy Ghost to be with me and help guide me. My days are different when this happens and I am quickly reminded how much I need His constant companionship. We need to seek the Spirit, live for the Spirit, work for the Spirit, pray for the Spirit, and do all we can to call upon the Holy Spirit to be our constant companion!

> Here we bow in meek devotion;
> Here we sing God's holy praise.
> Here our hearts, with fond emotion,
> Seek to learn his holy ways.[31]

There are some great scriptures that get the message across regarding *seeking!* These scriptures can teach us more than I can. I love the promise in the *Book of Mormon* in 1 Nephi 10: 19 that reads, "For he that diligently seeketh shall find: and the mysteries of God shall be unfolded unto them, by the power of the Holy Ghost...."

Also, *Doctrine and Covenants* 88:63 reads, "Seek me diligently and ye shall find me." When I look up the word "diligently" in the Merriam-Webster dictionary, it says: "characterized by steady, earnest, and energetic effort." This prompts me to do a self-evaluation. Am I diligent in seeking the Holy Ghost in my life? I know in the last few years, I have made a more earnest effort to call upon the Holy Ghost to be with me and help me. I appreciate the promise in the scripture in 1 Nephi that "the mysteries of God shall be unfolded" unto them. In my professional work, I am constantly trying to help under-served (from homeless families to refugees to seniors and more) populations that do not have dental insurance find access to dental care. There are so many barriers to making this happen. As I have called upon the Holy Ghost to lead me to resources, miraculous doors have been opened! As I rely on the Holy Ghost and the resources that He leads me to, I feel synergy in addressing these issues! ☺

"The Holy Ghost is a reminder and will bring to our remembrance the things which we have learned and which we need in the time thereof. He is an inspirer and will put words in our mouths, enlighten our understandings and direct our thoughts. He is a testifier and will bear record to us of the divinity of the Father and the Son and of their missions and of the program which they have given us. He is a teacher and will increase our knowledge. He is a companion and will walk with us, inspiring us all along the way, guiding our footsteps, impeaching our weaknesses, strengthening our resolves, and revealing to us righteous aims and purposes."[32]

One Sling—Surround Yourself with Positive People

Although David needed only the one stone to conquer Goliath, he was prepared with both the stones and his sling to conquer Goliath. I've shared what my five stones are. Now I'd like to share a sling that is important in my life. Without it I wouldn't be able to use my five stones as effectively.

Although there have been many 'spiritual' slings that have helped me in my life, there is one that has truly affected the course of my life and this *is to be around associations that are uplifting around me!* In my patriarchal blessing, I am counseled to "have associations that are uplifting around me." This has been super valuable and sort of like an offensive approach. It is a proactive way of building your spiritual and emotional support team! These are some of my life-long best friends from my home state of Oregon. They are angels in my life—my wonderful uplifting associations the Lord has blessed me with! ☺

It has also helped me stay in check to be the person that is uplifting to others. Are there people in your life that put down others? Are there people in your life that are toxic? Always complaining about life? Or use bad language a lot or talk about others behind their back? Do you have friends or family that want to go to the temple? Serve others? Are kind to others? Listen without judgment? Think about who is in your life—do they bring you closer to Christ, or invite a bad or toxic spirit into your life?

I'm grateful for David's wonderful example of how he conquered Goliath! Let us ascend and upgrade our life to be ready to face our modern day Goliaths armed with

God's power! I have experienced for myself that as we live with gratitude, increase the meaningfulness of our personal prayers, attend the temple, take opportunities to serve others, and *daily* seek the power of the Holy Ghost in our life, we can conquer today's Goliaths! At a BYU devotional, Kent F. Richards shared this regarding waiting with purpose:

> "Faithful, patient waiting implies that we strive daily to do the little things: daily scripture study, no matter our schedules; daily prayers with hearts drawn out always; daily worthiness for the companionship of the Holy Ghost; and daily diligence to keep our environment fit for the Spirit. Are you waiting for external circumstance to compel you to action? Are you waiting to be perfectly assured of the end before you dare begin? Are you waiting upon the Lord or sometimes just waiting until you graduate or marry or begin a family or qualify for life's work before you fully commit? When does your ministry begin? Is it now?"[33]

A final challenge I will give to each of us is to pray to know how best to *consecrate your waits* in life! Pray to know how best to fulfill the measure of your creation! Don't compare yourself to what others are doing! Whatever your limits are, God will reach your reaching! God knows YOU by name and speaks your name often! The Holy Ghost is a beautiful companion and gift that we can call upon to guide and direct us. BELIEVE THIS! May we have the courage to be all HE wants and needs us to be and find joy in living an abundant life! ☺

THESE ARE MORE ANGELS IN MY LIFE!

NOTES

1. Jeffrey R. Holland, "The Ministry of Angels," *Ensign*, November 2008, 31

2. Donald W. Parry, "Angles, Chariots, and the Lord of Host," BYU Devotionals, July 21, 2012

3. Jeffrey R. Holland, "For a Wise Purpose," *Ensign*, January 1996, 17

4. Neal A. Maxwell, "Jesus, the Perfect Mentor," *Ensign*, February 2001, 8

5. Paraphrased from the hymn http://www.hymntime. com/tch/htm/l/o/v/loveofgo.htm

6. Neal A. Maxwell, All These Things Shall Give Thee Experience, Salt Lake City, Deseret Book 1980, 46

7. Dieter F. Uchtdorf, "The Love of God," *Ensign*, November 2009

8. Jeffrey R. Holland, "The Ministry of Angels," *Ensign*, November 2008

9. President Dieter F. Uchtdorf, "Come, Join with Us," *Ensign*, November 2013, 23

10. Ezra T. Benson, "The Constitution—A Heavenly Banner," BYU Devotional Talk, September 16, 1986

11. Ezra T. Benson, "The Constitution—A Heavenly Banner," BYU Devotional Talk, September 16, 1986

12. www.nps.gov/wori/learn/historyculture/grimke-sisters.htm

13. http://ngm.nationalgeographic.com/ngm/0309/feature1/

14. Ezra T. Benson, "A Marvelous Work and a Wonder," *Ensign*, May 1980, 67

15. Ezra T. Benson, Teachings of Presidents of the Church, Chapter 9: The Book of Mormon—Keystone of Our Religion, 30-32

16. Spencer W. Kimball, "The What and Why and How of Bearing a Testimony," June 2016 *Ensign*, 80

17. Michelle Martin, "Who Am I Really?" *New Era*, August 2010, 45

18. John McCain with Mark Salter, A Family Memoir Faith of My Fathers, Random House, 1999, 254

19. Marjorie Pay Hinckley, "Glimpses into the Life and Heart of Marjorie Pay Hinckley," Editor Virginia H. Pearce, 1

20. Neal A. Maxwell, "The Great Plan of the Eternal God," *Ensign*, May 1984, 22

21. David A. Bednar, "The Tender Mercies of the Lord," *Ensign*, May 2005

22. David A. Bednar, "The Tender Mercies of the Lord," *Ensign*, May 2005

23. Joseph B. Wirthlin, "Come What May, and Love It," *Ensign*, November 2008, 26-28

24. Elaine S. Dalton, "A Return to Virtue," *Ensign*, November 2008, 78

25. Gordon B. Hinckley, "Overpowering the Goliaths in Our Lives," *Ensign*, January 2002

26. *Book of Mormon*, Moroni 10:3

27. http://www.usnews.com/news/articles/2008/01/28/ john-mccain-prisoner-of-war-a-first-person-account

28. Neal A. Maxwell, The Neal A. Maxwell Quote Book, 339

29. Teachings of the Presidents of the Church: Howard W. Hunter, Melchizedek Priesthood and Relief Society Course of Study, 2015-2016, 179

30. Teachings of the Presidents of the Church: Howard W. Hunter, Melchizedek Priesthood and Relief Society Course of Study, 2015-2016, 183

31. "Welcome, Welcome, Sabbath Morning" The Church of Jesus Christ of Latter-Day Saints, Hymn No. 280

32. Gerald N. Lund, "In Tune The Role of the Spirit in Teaching and Learning," Deseret Book, Salt Lake City, 2013, 17, Quoting Teachings of Spencer W. Kimball, Edited by Edward L. Kimball, 1982, 23

33. Kent F. Richards, "Lessons from the Savior's Young Adult Life," BYU Devotionals, March 10, 2015

ABOUT THE AUTHOR

Michelle L. Martin was raised in Portland, Oregon. She joined the Church of Jesus Christ of Latter-Day Saints at the age of seventeen. Later, Michelle served an LDS mission in the Illinois Peoria Mission. Michelle received a Bachelor's Degree in Dental Hygiene from Weber State University, and a Master's Degree in Public Health from the University of Utah. Currently, Michelle works at the Utah Department of Health as the Oral Health Specialist for the state of Utah. She works with and cares for under-served populations and helps them get access to dental care. She also is the Co-Dental Director for the Utah Special Olympics dental screenings. One of Michelle's loves in life has been traveling abroad on humanitarian trips to provide oral hygiene and dental care. She has been to the Marshall Islands, Vietnam, Peru, Guatemala, and Honduras. This is her second book, following after *Learning to Trust in the Lord*.

CPSIA information can be obtained
at www.ICGtesting.com
Printed in the USA
FSOW02n1643111116
27166FS